The Enchanted Forest
The Magical Lore of Trees

By Yvonne Aburrow

CAPALL BANN PUBLISHING

The Enchanted Forest
The Magical Lore of Trees

ISBN 1 898307 08 3

First printed 1993
Reprinted Jan 1994
Reprinted Oct 1994
Reprinted July 1995
Reprinted Dec 1995

Published by:

Capall Bann Publishing
Freshfields
Chieveley
Berks
RG20 8TF

Tel/Fax 01635 248711

CONTENTS

The Oak King
and
The Holly King

INTRODUCTION

From earliest times, trees have been the object of veneration and wonder. It began with particular trees whose spirits were venerated; some became deities. Balder, god of the oak and mistletoe, began in this way; so did Zeus, Jupiter, Thor, Donar, Thunor, Perkunas (all deities of the oak and thunder), and numerous others. Even today magical powers are ascribed to trees; on an airbase in Cambridgeshire during the Gulf War the wives of absent pilots tied ribbons to a tree on the base, for good luck. They probably did not know that this was an ancient folk custom: it arose spontaneously in response to their need.

Recently trees and woods have been in the news due to the expansion of the road-building programme. Seven of the Donga tribe have been imprisoned for breaking the injunction against them returning to Twyford Down, where the M3 extension has made a hideous scar in the Hampshire countryside, destroying wildlife habitats, sites of special scientific interest, and archaeological sites forever. I visited the Dongas back in April, and found a genuine bunch of people trying to save all this in the face of persecution from the road-builders, who had physically assaulted them, and sexually assaulted the women among them. The occupation of the hillside by the Dongas will leave no physical marks, because they recycle their rubbish and use as little packaging as possible. A sign near the communal bender said "No radios or cassette players; no toilet paper, use a spade". Their courage, however, will be remembered.

The good news is that Oxleas Wood has been saved from a similar fate, thanks to the various people who have protested against its destruction; but now the Department of Transport is threatening to widen the M25 from 6 to 14 lanes, destroying more woodland; and Wychbury Hill, a sacred site in the West Midlands, is under threat from similar development. A list of organisations protesting against the destruction of the environment is printed in Appendix A.

On a wider scale, the destruction of the rainforests proceeds, despite calls for their preservation, if only to ensure a continuing supply of oxygen for the planet. The rainforests contain huge numbers of as yet undiscovered plants and trees, which may contain cures for diseases; they are inhabited by fauna of great beauty, whose survival is essential for eco-diversity and the food-chain; and people live there whose lifestyle and spiritual heritage may be of vital importance to the rest of the planet. The number of folk beliefs about and medicinal uses for trees in this book attests to this.

Forests are places of beauty and serenity, but also wildness and savagery. Much of the British Isles was once covered in forest, and although the clearing of some of the forest resulted in other habitats, such as moor and heathland, it is possible to lose too much woodland. Many species of flora and fauna have become extinct owing to deforestation.

The poetry, mythology, and folklore of many countries reflects an enduring fascination with the forest. To the Celts, it was the Enchanted Forest, a place of testing and initiation, the threshold of the soul, the realm of death and the unknown; to the Hindus, it is a place of retreat from the world, a source of peace and spiritual tranquillity, and a place for contemplation.

Trees, on the other hand, have been in many cultures the image of the cosmos. In Buddhism, Buddha is equated with the cosmic pillar and the tree of life; in Kabbalah, the Ets Chayyim or Tree of Life is the body of Adam Kadmon, the cosmic man; to the Norse peoples the cosmic tree was Yggdrasil, Odin's horse; to the Saxons it was Irmensul; and the maypole, found in many cultures, also represents the cosmic pillar.

In addition, folk medicine has always relied on Nature's pharmacopeia of trees and other plants. Obvious examples includethe willow tree, from which salicylic acid, the active ingredient of aspirin, is derived.

Plants are also a source of psychotropic substances; some shamans may have used alcohol as such. The word cider is probably derived from seidr, a Germanic word meaning 'to heat', i.e. to induce an altered state. (The word shaman is derived from a Sanskrit word also meaning 'to heat'.) Before the introduction of cultivated apple species, cider would have been made from crab apples; the yeasts growing on the skins of these would probably have had somewhat unpredictable effects. At Delphi, the priestesses of Apollo chewed laurel leaves to induce prophetic trances.

Trees have also been used in magic since time immemorial, both for healing and protection, as well as other more dubious purposes. Their practical applications often incorporate their magical properties; for example the use of oak for doors and birch for cradles. The lore of trees is a fascinating and multifarious subject, constantly weaving in and out from one culture to another, reflecting the preoccupations of human beings from one age to another.

In this book I have tried to collect as much information as possible relating to trees; botanical information, magical uses, medicinal uses, folklore, weather lore, mythology, rhymes and songs, sayings and poems, craft uses and culinary uses. I spent a long time waiting for such a book to appear; when it didn't, I decided to write one myself.

Yvonne Aburrow   August 1993 C.E.

II

ACKNOWLEDGEMENTS

Thanks to Stewart, for encouragement and the gift of a computer; Patrick, for helpful suggestions and the loan of useful books; my mother, for imparting to me her botanical knowledge and her enthusiasm for flowers, trees, birds, and animals; Britt, for the loan of useful books; Holger Jordan, for the German elder song and the "Zu fallen einen schonen Baum..." rhyme; Capall Bann, for their helpful and friendly approach to publishing; and Prudence Jones and Nigel Pennick, for information on geomancy, town layouts, etc.

Illustrations

Cover design and illustrations on pages 36, 61, 109, 112, 139, 178 and 183 by Gill Bent.
All other illustrations by the author.

Horse Chestnut

IV

CHAPTER ONE:
MYTHOLOGY, SYMBOLISM, AND FOLK CUSTOMS

Very old are the woods;
And the buds that break
Out of the briar's boughs,
When March winds wake,
So old with their beauty are -
Oh, no man knows
Through what wild centuries
Roves back the rose.

(Walter de la Mare, "All That's Past")

Trees are potent sources of symbolism: leaves, fruit, twigs, nuts, and boughs all have their own symbolism. The tree itself has various meanings, and folk customs and myths have arisen involving trees: the Sacral King, the maypole, the bonfire, the needfire; tree spirits (from the dryad to the yaksa), deities of trees, and people transformed into trees.

The Sacral King

In "The Golden Bough", J. G. Frazer explores the mythology of the Sacral King. One version of this was the priest-king in the wood at Nemi, who stood under the sacred tree. Challengers for the kingship would fight him; if he was killed, the challenger would replace him. He was traditionally an escaped slave. Another version of this is the cycle of the Oak King (King of the Waxing Year) and the Holly King (King of the Waning Year). At Yule, the Oak King (Jupiter or Balder) kills the Holly King (Saturn or Hodur); at Midsummer the resurrected Holly King kills the Oak King. This theme is explored in great detail in "The White Goddess" by Robert Graves.

There is a theory that William Rufus, who was killed by an arrow in the New Forest while out hunting 'on the morrow of Lammas' died as a sacral king, for the renewal of the land. Whether this is so or not, it is significant that he died at Lammas, the traditional date for the death of the Corn King.

The sacral king in the form of the Dying God is always killed on a tree. Examples are Christ and Odin; there is even an amulet of Orpheus crucified with the moon and stars beneath his feet, probably carved by an initiate of one of the mystery cults which flourished in the first two centuries of the modern era.

The Maypole

The maypole is the axis mundi around which the universe revolves. The tree, stripped of its foliage which symbolises change, becomes the changeless axis or centre. The pole itself is phallic; the discus at the top from which the ribbons are suspended represents the feminine principle; the union of the two in the maypole represents fertility. The seven ribbons are the colours of the rainbow.

Originally the maypole was the sacred pine of Attis which was taken in procession or on a chariot to the temple of Cybele, where it was set up to be venerated. It was followed in the procession by men, women, and children, and dances were held round it.

Later this ceremony appeared in the Roman Hilaria, the Spring Festival, and then in the May Day celebrations of the May Queen and the Green Man, the spirit of vegetation.The ribbons of the maypole possibly derive from the bands of wool wrapped round the Attis pine. The entire ceremony is symbolic of renewed life, sexual union, resurrection, and spring.

The Green Man

In Sweden the maypole is erected on Midsummer's Eve; elsewhere it is erected on May Eve or Beltane (31st April). In Cornwall and Northamptonshire it was the custom to erect a may tree outside every house, and to deck the porches with hawthorn and sycamore. In Germany the maypole is generally a tall pine stripped of its branches; in Sweden it is a spruce; everywhere it is decked with ribbons, flowers, painted eggshells, and bunting. In 1583 the Puritan writer Philip Stubbes railed against the bringing in of the maypole from the woods, accompanied by much mirth and revelry. The overnight ceremonies in the wood involved much deflowering of virgins.

In some parts of Europe, young men would erect a may tree outside the home of their sweetheart. Dancing around the pole was almost universal; in some places there was a race on foot or on horseback to the foot of the maypole. In all these cases the custom was to bring in a new maypole every year. This has lapsed in some places, where a permanent maypole has been erected, but there is little doubt that the original practice was to bring in a new pole every year, representing that year's incarnation of the vegetation spirit.

In parts of Russia the old maypole was thrown into the river after three days, perhaps as a rain charm; in many places the old tree was burnt after a year; just as many people keep their palm crosses from Palm Sunday for a year and then burn them. In many places a person or effigy is regarded as the embodiment of the May alongside the may tree or pole. Sometimes there is a May King, more often a May Queen, sometimes a bridegroom and bride. In Scotland it is still the custom for people to wash their faces in the dew on May morning.

At Thann, in Alsace, a girl called the Little May Rose, dressed in white, carries a small may-tree decked with garlands and ribbons. Her companions collect gifts from door to door, and sing:

> Little May Rose turn round three times,
> Let us look at you round and round!
> Rose of the May, come to the greenwood away,
> We will be merry all.
> So we go from the May to the Roses.

The produce of the year depends on giving to the May singers, for the song continues, expressing a wish that those who give nothing will have their fowls eaten by martens, their vines will not bear, their trees will bear no nuts, and their fields no corn.

The Moon Tree

The moon tree is a symbol of the Great Mother; it is a curious combination of the cosmic axis and the tree spirit - the trunk represents the body of the Great Mother, which gives birth to the Dying God or Sacral King, then reabsorbs him in death. It is sometimes depicted as a pillar or truncated tree, sometimes as a growing tree with the moon in its branches. In Assyro-Babylonian depictions of the moon tree, a winged lion and unicorn attend the tree. The winged lion is the waxing moon, the tree is the full moon, and the unicorn is the waning moon. The truncated tree is the Great

3

Moon-tree climbing a trellis surmounted by torches, which are an attribute of Moon deities.

Moon tree

Mother; a statue of Attis was tied to a truncated pine at the annual festival of his death and resurrection; Osiris' body was enclosed in a tree trunk; Christ was crucified on a truncated tree (pagan art often represented the moon tree in the form of a cross surmounting a crescent moon, a symbol which is still found in Greek churches). The ribbons of the maypole and the lights on the Christmas tree represent new life being given to the tree. The moon tree is often represented with Sinn, the Babylonian moon-god.

The Hymn of Eridu describes the moon tree as the beautiful house of the moon, ruling over the earth, the heavens, and the underworld. Eridu was the centre of an ancient civilisation on the borders of the Persian Gulf; it was possibly here that the Chaldeans originated.

The Hymn of Eridu

Its root of white crystal stretched towards the deep.
Its seat was the central place of the earth;
Its foliage was the couch of Ziku, the primeval mother.
Into the heart of the holy house which spreads its shade like a forest
hath no man entered,
There is [the house of] the mighty mother,
            who passes across the sky;
In the midst of it was Tammuz.

The fertilising power of the moon was seen as fire; this power is hidden in wood or
tree, sleeping or latent, and can be drawn out by rubbing, the "primitive" way of
producing fire. In India, Agni, the fire god, is seen as hidden in the sacred wood from
which he is reborn by the friction of the fire stick.

The moon tree is also associated with Soma; Indian myth tells us that the Gods drank
the Soma of the heavenly tree, thereby gaining immortality (see the information on
the Fly Agaric mushroom under BIRCH). The Hindu women of Maharashtra,
whenever the New Moon falls on Somavara (Monday, the moon-day), celebrate the
rite of soma-vati, dancing round the sacred fig tree.

Green George

In Russia and other Slavic countries the personification of the vegetation spirit is
called Green George, a leaf-clad youth appearing on St. George's Day (23rd April)
bearing gifts and followed by girls singing. This custom is also prevalent among
Hungarian Gypsies.·

Robin Hood

Robin Hood may have been a real person, or more than one person; certainly the
archetype of the outlaw is very ancient. Robin Hood is the lord of the forest, the wild
and untameable one. His consort Marian represents the Goddess, and their union is a
symbol of fertility, the renewal of the land.

Merry, merry England is waking as of old,
With eyes of blither hazel and hair of brighter gold:
For Robin Hood is here again beneath the bursting spray
In Sherwood, in Sherwood, about the break of day.

Love is in the greenwood building him a house
Of wild rose and hawthorn and honeysuckle boughs:
Love is in the greenwood: dawn is in the skies;
And Marian is waiting with a glory in her eyes.

(from "Sherwood", by Alfred Noyes)

Noyes is best known for his poem "The Highwayman" - another outlaw archetype.
People take these legendary outlaws to their hearts because they represent the nomad
and subversive in all of us - they are archetypes of the wild and the free.

Needfires

When there was an outbreak of plague or cattle disease, people in Germany, England,
Scotland, and the Slavonic countries would kindle a needfire.
In "The Way of Wyrd" by Brian Bates, Wulf the sorcerer kindles a needfire by
pushing a polished hazel twig stripped of its bark through a hole drilled with a knife
in an oak stake until the wand catches fire, whereupon he pushes it into a pile of dry
kindling. "This is wildfire... Wood on wood, built from the substance it consumes."

The method related in "The Golden Bough" consists of a greased pole being passed
rapidly back and forth through two stakes with holes in them, or being rolled in the
holes by means of a rope attached to either end and being pulled back and forth.
Sometimes a cartwheel (which must be new) formed part of the mechanism.

Taboos surrounding the needfire varied. In most places all fires other than the
needfire had to be extinguished; various taboos existed concerning the purity and
relationship of the kindlers (must be twins, must have the same name, must be
brothers, must be virgins, or must be married men - it differed from one place to
another).

When all was ready, the cattle were driven through the fire to protect them from the
plague. Afterwards people ran through the embers and smeared each other with
ashes. In some places two fires were kindled and the cattle driven between them.

Bonfires

Bonfires were a fertility custom, for example burning straw houses or effigies to ensure an abundant harvest, and to keep mildew, blight, and hail from the crops. The custom was observed all over Europe in various forms and at various festivals (Easter, Beltane, Midsummer, etc.). In Belgium people used to jump over the Midsummer bonfire to prevent colic. In Wales 3 or 9 different kinds of wood and charred faggots from the previous year's bonfire were used. The fire was generally lit on rising ground. Amongst witches it is the custom to leap over the Bel-fire at Beltane; couples leap it hand in hand. In many parts of Europe a burning cartwheel (a symbol of the sun) was pushed downhill, often at Midsummer to symbolise the ensuing shortening of the daylight hours. St. Catherine, whose symbol is a burning wheel, is possibly a continuation of a pagan sun-goddess. The Royston Cave in Hertfordshire has a carving of St. Catherine holding a wheel with eight spokes (the eight festivals?), and there is a hill named after her near Winchester (next to Twyford Down).

Effigies burnt in bonfires generally represent the tree spirit or spirit of vegetation. The burning of effigies of Guy Fawkes on Bonfire night probably has its origin in this much older custom, since Bonfire Night is celebrated not long after Hallowe'en, the final harvest festival. (Lammas is the corn harvest, Autumn Equinox the fruit harvest, and Hallowe'en or Samhain the day on which surplus cattle were killed to be salted down for the winter.)

The Forest

The forest is the realm of the psyche and the feminine principle, a place of testing and initiation, of unknown perils and darkness. It is the underworld, the abode of the dead. In Norse mythology, one of the twelve dwellings of the gods was Ydalir, valley of yews, where Uller received the souls of the dead. Entering the Dark Forest or the Enchanted Forest is a threshold symbol. The soul enters the perils of the unknown, the realm of death, the secrets of nature or the spiritual world.

The forest can also represent lack of spiritual insight and light, humanity lost in the darkness without divine direction. Hence the expression, "We're not out of the woods yet..."

Retreat into the forest is a symbolic death before the rebirth of initiation. To the Hindus the forest dweller is one who has left the active world for a life of contemplation, who has 'died' to this world.

In Druidic legend the sun and the forest are married as male and female, light and darkness.

> "O the rising of the sun,
> And the running of the deer..."

In Australia, the Aborigines view the forest as the Beyond, the realm of shades, and the place of initiation. In Shamanistic lore, it is the dwelling of the spirits.

In Roman mythology the gods of the forest were Silvanus, son of a shepherd of Sybaris and a she-goat, and Vertumnus (from Latin vertere, to change), god of fruit trees, who successfully seduced Pomona by disguising himself as an old woman. In addition, Flora was the goddess of the vine, fruit-trees, and flowers.

In Greece the temples of Demeter, called Megara, were often built in the forest.

In Assyro-Babylonian myth the forest, full of cedars, was the abode of the gods and the sanctuary of Irnini (possibly a form of Ishtar) but it was also the dwelling place of the monster Khumbaba. It is significant that the first part of the Epic of Gilgamesh describes Gilgamesh's and Enkidu's journey into the forest to confront this monster - truly an initiatory journey.

Wood

Wood represents the wholeness of the primordial, paradisal state, being that which gives shelter at birth and death, in the cradle and the coffin. It also forms the marriage bed, the gallows tree, the cross and the ship of the dead, the lunar barque. Among the Norsemen, a hanged man was a sacrifice to Odin, because Odin hung on the world tree Yggdrasil to obtain wisdom.

Wood is the prima materia of the East, hence Christ as a carpenter: the carpenter uses tools symbolic of the divine attribute of bringing order out of chaos. In Hindu and Tibetan symbolism wood is the material from which all things were shaped.

> "Brahman was the wood, Brahman the tree from which they shaped heaven and earth" (Taittirya Brahmana).

In Chinese thought wood is one of the Five Elements, representing Spring, the East, and the colours blue and green.

The Tree

The tree represents the whole of manifestation, the synthesis of earth and water, and dynamic life. It is both imago mundi and axis mundi, joining the three worlds (heaven, earth, and underworld) and making communication between them possible. It gives access to the power of the sun; it is also an omphalos, a centre of dragon energy or cthonic power. It is the feminine principle, nourishing, sheltering, and protecting; trees are often depicted as female figures. As the world axis it is linked with the mountain and the pillar. The world tree is rooted in the depths of the earth at the centre of the world, and grows into the realm of Time, its branches representing differentiation on the plane of manifestation.

Evergreen trees symbolise immortality and the undying spirit, and are often used in funerary and mourning rites to remind mourners of the resurrection or reincarnation to come (depending on your religious beliefs). See BOX, CYPRESS, YEW.

Assyro-Babylonian Tree of Life, Bas-relief from the North-West Palace of Nimrud c. 900 B.C.E.

Deciduous trees represent renewal, regeneration, death and rebirth, resurrection, reproduction, and the life principle.

The Tree of Life and the Tree of Knowledge grow in Paradise. The Tree of Life is at the centre and signifies regeneration and the return to the state of primordial perfection. In the Garden of Eden myth, God casts Adam and Eve out of the garden

9

lest they eat of the fruit of the Tree of Life, and live forever. The Tree of Knowledge is dualistic, giving the knowledge of good and evil.

The inverted tree is a magical tree; the roots in the air and branches in the earth represent inverted action, that which is on high descending below and that which is below ascending on high. It is the principle of "as above, so below", the reflection of the celestial and terrestrial worlds in each other.

Egyptian Tree of Life (adapted from a wall painting c. 1300 B.C.E.

A tree with a serpent appears in many cultures. The tree is the cosmic axis; the serpent coiled round it is the cycles of manifestation. The same is true of the caduceus, Hermes' staff. Alternatively the serpent is the guardian of the tree, signifying the difficulty of getting wisdom, as in the case of the serpent Ladon which guarded the tree on which the Golden Apples of the Hesperides grew; or it may tempt the man or woman into eating the forbidden fruit, as in the Garden of Eden myth.

A tree with a stone and an altar is the moon tree. Often depicted with the moon, the tree symbolises the principle of change, the stone the principle of stasis. In ancient times, the body of a woman was the altar of the gods.

Climbing trees symbolises the ascent from one plane to another (e.g. achieving gnosis, ascending the Tree of Life in the Kabbalah).

In Chinese legend, the Tree of Sweet Dew, or Singing Tree, grows on top of the sacred mountain at the centre of the world.

In Arab symbolism, the Zodiac is represented as a tree with twelve branches, on which the stars are the fruits.

In Hindu mythology, the Cosmic Tree springs from the Cosmic Egg. The Aditi is the Tree of Life, the essence of individuality; whilst the Diti is the Tree of Knowledge and Samsara. The Adityas are the twelve signs of the zodiac, represented as a tree bearing twelve suns. The Trimurti is a triple tree with three suns, representing the Three Powers: either Siva as Creator, Preserver, and Destroyer; or Brahma as Creator, Vishnu as Preserver, and Siva as Destroyer.

15th century Indian Tree of Life

To the Iranians, the Cosmic Tree has seven branches: the seven metals, the seven planets, and sevenfold history. In alchemy, the seven metals correspond to the seven planets as follows:

Sun	Gold
Moon	Silver
Venus	Copper
Mars	Iron
Mercury	Quicksilver
Jupiter	Tin
Saturn	Lead

In Zoroastrian thought, there are two trees: the Tree of the Solar Eagle, which sprang from the primordial ocean, and the Tree of All Seeds, whose seeds are the germs of all living things.

In Islam, the olive tree is the Tree of Blessing, giving the world the light of Allah; there is a Celestial Tree at the centre of Paradise; and a lote tree marks the impassable boundary. There is also an inverted tree of happiness which has its roots in highest heaven and spreads its branches - and its blessing - over the earth.

The Japanese Bonsai tree represents the austerity and wisdom of Nature.

In Mexican legend, the cosmic tree is the agave cactus, depicted with a falcon representing the power of the sun or the liberation of the new moon.

Twigs

The barsom twigs of the Parsees, bound in a bundle, represent the 'bundle of life' - individual lives bound together in unity.

In the Anglo- Saxon Nine herbs charm, reference is made to 'glory twigs' (wuldortanas), nine in number (nine being the sacred number, the number of the worlds in the cosmos):

> "A worm came crawling, it killed nothing
> For Woden took nine glory twigs
> He smote the adder that it flew into nine parts.
> There apple brought this to pass against poison,
> That she never more would enter her house."

Fruit

Fruit symbolises immortality, the essence, the culmination of one state and the seed of the next.

"First fruits" are the best of that which is sacrificed; hence Christ was the First Fruit of the Virgin Mary.

The fruit of the tree of passion signifies attachment to the world; the fruit of the Tree of Knowledge is the symbol of the fall, self-consciousness as being separate from God, the Universal All.

The fruit of the Tree of Life symbolises immortality; fruit and flowers together are funerary offerings. Fruit carrried by Priapus signifies fertility. The image of Priapus was often erected in orchards and gardens, both to protect them and encourage their growth.

Leaves

Leaves symbolise fertility. growth, and renewal. Green leaves depict hope, revival, and renewal, whilst dead leaves depict sadness, Autumn, and decay. Crowns of leaves symbolise divinity or triumph and victory.

In Chinese symbolism the leaves of the Cosmic Tree represent all beings in the universe: the Ten Thousand Things.

Tripartite leaves represent trinities, triads, and the phallic principle. (See IVY, VINE, and FIG.)

Nuts

Nuts symbolise hidden wisdom, fertility, and longevity. They are associated with the Great Mother, the kernel being the Divine Child within the womb.

Hazel nuts represent peace and lovers; in Irish legend the salmon of Connla fed on the hazel nuts which dropped into the pool from the tree above, bestowing wisdom.

Walnuts were served at Greek and Roman weddings as a symbol of fertility and longevity.

Acorns

Acorns represent potential for growth, the Cosmic Egg. They were a Scandinavian and Celtic symbol of life, fecundity, and immortality, sacred to Thor.

Cones

The pine cone symbolises fecundity and good fortune. Also called the Heart of Bacchus, it is an attribute of Dionysos, and an emblem of Serapis, Cybele, Astarte at Byblos in Phoenicia, and Artemis in Pamphylia. It is phallic, and also represents the spiral generative and creative force. The white cone is an emblem of Aphrodite.

Resin and Sap

Resin represents immortality and incorruptibility. Resin-producing trees share the symbolism of evergreens (see above). Both resin and sap are regarded as being the soul of the tree, and a source of fire and hence regeneration. Resin is also seen as the tears of the Great Mother - Freyja was said to have shed tears of amber at the death of Svipdag.

Sap signifies the life-force, vitality, strength, and blood; a sap-filled plant represents motherhood; being full of sap signifies vitality and youthfulness, but also giddy irresponsibility.

Boughs

The Tree of Life and fertility can be depicted by a branch, hence it was a bridal symbol. Boughs decorating the house and 'bringing home the may' (going to cut a hawthorn branch on May 1st) was a spring fertility rite.

The Golden Bough is the link between this world and the next, the passport to the heavenly world. It symbolises initiation and the magic wand. It enabled Aeneas to pass through the underworld and survive. The priest of Diana's sacred grove at Nemi won his office by killing his predecessor with the Golden Bough (hence the title of J. G. Frazer's classic work).

The Silver Bough, the apple, is the link between this world and the faery realm, Tir nan og. Breaking the bough means the death of a king. The bough is also related to the symbolism of the wand, pole, and oar.

To the Celts the bough symbolised the renewal of youth; the Druids held the mistletoe (q.v.) sacred as the Golden Bough. In Hebrew myth, the sacred wood of the acacia is sometimes referred to as the Golden Bough.

The Wand

The wand is a conductor of power and supernatural force; the attribute of shamans, witches, and magicians. The Wand of Hypnos confers sleep and forgetfulness. The Gaelic white wand was made of yew; the Celtic wand was made of hazel.

14

The Pole

The pole is the world axis (see Maypole), the cosmic centre, the still point at the heart of everything. It is a stabilising force, the tree of life without its branches, which represent change, growth, and manifestation. It is phallic, representing fertility and procreation. Fixed on the Pole Star, it upholds the heavens, and the firmament revolves around it.

The Oar

The oar represents power, skill, and knowledge. It is the rod or spear which stirs the Primordial Ocean (the Womb of the Great Mother); it is also the pole which guides the Ship of the Dead across the waters of death to the other shore. In Egypt the oar represented sovereignty, action, and rule (guiding the ship of state). It is generally an attribute of river gods.

Boats

The boat is the yoni, the female creative principle. Female figureheads are lunar, and a ship with one of these represents a womb or cradle - the feminine vessel of transformation, and a saviour and protector on the sea of life. The mast represents the cosmic pillar; the tiller and the rudder share the symbolism of the oar, which guides the ship of state. The moon and the sun were envisaged as being carried across the sea in boats (such as Osiris' boat Millions of Years, in which he sails as the Man in the Moon), and the earth was seen as a boat floating on the primordial waters.

The Cradle

The cradle is seen as the cosmic barque, the ship of life rocking on the primordial ocean. It symbolises new life, a fresh beginning. It is made of wood (q.v.), which gives shelter at birth, during life, and in death.

CHAPTER TWO:
THE TREE AS COSMIC AXIS

The one had leaves of dark green that beneath were as shining silver, and from each of his countless flowers a dew of silver light was ever falling, and the earth beneath was dappled with the shadows of his fluttering leaves. The other bore leaves of a young green like the new-opened beech; their edges were of glittering gold. Flowers swung upon her branches in clusters of yellow flame, formed each to a glowing horn that spilled a golden rain upon the ground; and from the blossom of that tree there came warmth and a great light.

(J. R. R. Tolkien, description of Telperion and Laurelin, in "The Silmarillion")

The cosmologies of many cultures represent the tree as world axis. I shall examine some of them in detail.

Tree of Life (Ets Chayyim)

The Kabbalistic Tree of Life was once represented as an actual tree. It is also the body of Adam Kadmon, the cosmic man. The Ets Chayyim is represented in modern Judaism by the Menorah, the seven branched candlestick.

The tree consists of ten Sephiroth or spheres and twenty-two pathways, which correspond to the letters of the Hebrew alphabet. The Sephiroth are as follows:

	Name	Meaning	Correspondence
1.	Kether	(Crown)	
2.	Chokhmah	(Wisdom)	Zodiac
3.	Binah	(Understanding)	Saturn
4.	Hesed	(Mercy)	Jupiter
5.	Gevurah	(Judgement)	Mars
6.	Tiphereth	(Beauty)	Sun
7.	Netzach	(Eternity)	Venus
8.	Hod	(Glory)	Mercury
9.	Yesod	(Foundation)	Moon
10.	Malkhut	(Kingdom)	Earth
	Daath	(Knowledge)	Holy Spirit (Ruach)

The Menorah

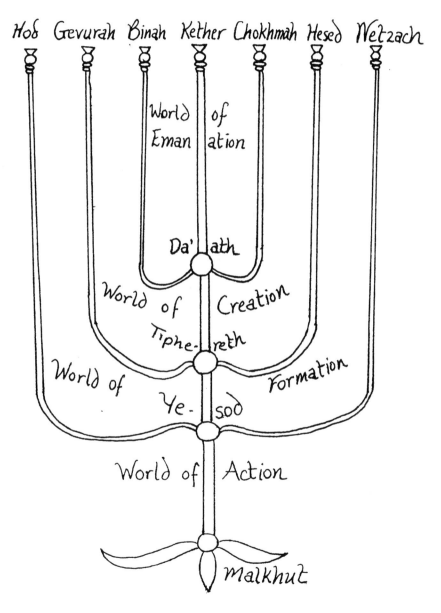

Hod   Gevurah   Binah   Kether   Chokhmah   Hesed   Netzach

World of Emanation

Da'ath

World of Creation

Tiphe-reth

World of Formation

World of

Ye-sod

World of Action

Malkhut

Tree of Life Ets Chayyim

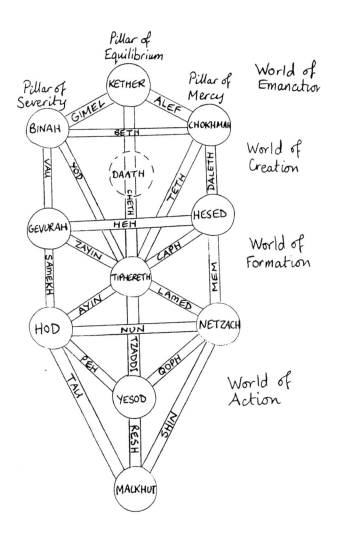

Adam Kadmon is the first manifestation of the Godhead on the material plane. His body is the Tree of Life, the ten Sephiroth representing the stages of the manifestation of God in the Creation. There are also four worlds: Aziluth (Proximity or Emanation); Beriah (Creation); Yezirah (Formation); and Asiyyah (Action). The soul must descend through these spheres in order to be made manifest. The tree grows downwards into the world from Kether, the crown.

For more information on the Kabbalah, the following books are recommended:

"Kabbalah: Tradition of Hidden Knowledge" and "Tree of Life" by Zev ben Shimon Halevi

"A Kabbalah for the modern world" by Migene Gonzales-Wippler

Yggdrasil and Irmensul

Yggdrasil is the Scandinavian Cosmic Tree, the Mighty Ash, the Ever Green, the fountain of life, eternal life, and immortality. The gods meet in council beneath its branches; its roots are in the depths of the underworld. The trunk passes through Middle Earth, and the branches are in the heavens. Thus the tree unites the three worlds. From its root rises the fountain Hvergelmir, the source of all rivers and of earthly time. The root is constantly attacked by the dragon Nidhogg, the Dread Biter, representing the malevolent forces of the universe. Odin's charger browses on the leaves, and in its boughs the eagle of light and the serpent of darkness are in perpetual conflict. The squirrel Ratatost, a mischief maker, carries insults from one to the other, creating strife between them.

In some legends Ratatost has a more constructive role as a messenger between the three worlds. There are four stags in the branches, representing the four winds, which browse on the leaves. The leaves are renewed by the attentions of the Three Norns or fates, who water the tree. The solar cock, symbolising vigilance, is sometimes depicted on the branches. Odin hung on the tree for nine nights and days to gain wisdom, and discovered the Runes. Shamans can travel the Bifrost or Rainbow Bridge, which connects Midgard and Asgard, and is guarded by Heimdall. Similarly, a bridge of ice, guarded by the goddess Mordgud, connects Midgard and Hel.

The nine worlds of Yggdrasil are:

Asgard	(abode of the Aesir pantheon)
Lightalfheim	(abode of the Light Elves)
Vanaheim	(abode of the Vanir pantheon)
Midgard	(Middle Earth)
Muspellheim	(realm of fire)
Nifelheim	(realm of fog)
Svartalfheim	(abode of the Dark Elves, or dwarves)
Jotunheim	(abode of the ice giants)
Hel	(realm of the dead)

The Well of Wyrd is in Asgard. The Three Norns dwell there, weaving the fate of humanity. They are Urd (fate), Skuld (being), and Verthandi (necessity). They nourish the tree, which is constantly decaying due to the various creatures which browse on it.

The well of Mimir, somewhere in Midgard, contains the oracular head of Mimir, a wise giant killed in battle. The well of Mimir is also a metaphor for the starry deeps of space and the night.

Odin hung on the world tree for nine days and nights to gain wisdom. Hanging on a tree was a shamanistic practice to induce altered states, hence the Tarot card of the Hanged Man, who is traditionally depicted with a serene expression and the crossed legs of the enlightened.

> I know that I hung on a windswept tree,
> Swung there nights all nine,
> Gashed with a blade,
> Bloodied for Odin,
> Myself an offering to myself -
> Knotted to that tree,
> That no man knows
> Whither the roots of it run.
>
> None gave me bread,
> None gave me drink;
> Down to the depths I peered
> To take up the Runes
> With a roaring scream
> And fell back in a dizzy swoon.   (Stanzas 138-139, The Havamal)

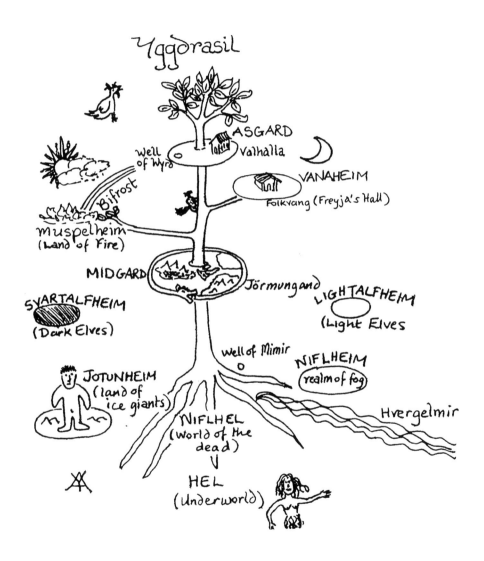

For more information about Norse cosmology and legend, "The Norse Myths" by Kevin Crossley-Holland is highly recommended reading.

Irmensul was the cosmic pillar of the Saxons. At the top is Hlidskjalf, the Air Throne of Woden, from which he can survey all the worlds. Next there is Asgard, abode of the gods, then Midgard or Middle Earth, then Utgard, the realm of the unmanifest and the souls of the wicked. Ermine Street, the ancient British road, is associated with Irmensul. Also the Saxons referred to the Milky Way as Irmin's Way or Irmin Street.

Other Cosmic Trees

In Buddhism, Buddha is equated with the Cosmic Pillar and the Tree of Life, represented by a pillar surmounted by a chakra (circle) representing the face of the sun.

Sakyamuni received his enlightenment whilst meditating under a fig tree (asvattha) or bodhi tree. The disciple Sariputra asked him in what form he should be venerated when he died, and the Buddha replied, "O Sariputra, when I have departed, my image should be cut in the shape of a fig tree." The original fig tree is located at Buddha Gaya.

The cosmic tree is also identified in India with Prajapati, the mythical ancestor of the world and of humanity, whose body consists of the three worlds of the universe: spiritual, heavenly, and earthly (svar, bhumas, bhin).

In Christianity, the Cross and the Tree of Life are equated with Christ, who is the fruit of that tree, which nourishes the Church. He is the New Adam, the redemption of the world.

St. Hippolytus wrote: "This wood is provided for my salvation... I establish myself in its roots, I lay myself down under its branches... Its fruit provides me with perfect joy... This tree goes up from the earth into the heavens... it is the plant of immortality, rising in the middle of heaven and earth - the firm prop of the universe, joining all things together..."

In the Dream of the Rood, probably written by the poet Cynewulf, the dreamer depicts Christ as "the young hero" who "mounted on the high cross, brave in the sight of many". This view is more nearly akin to the death of Odin than any Biblical account; it strongly resembles the Dying God theme of many cultures.

This tree of life imagery in Christianity is most probably derived from both the Northern Tradition and mystical Judaism. These strange bedfellows were brought together by the migration of Christianity from its heartland in the Mediterranean. Ideas from Islam also crept into Christendom via alchemy (from the Arabic alkimiya) and the contact made by the Templars and other mystical knights during the Crusades. Christian mystics also became interested in the Kabbalah around the time of the Renaissance (also the time when the Tarot was first standardised).

The maypole of folk tradition (discussed in Chapter One) also represents the cosmic axis. As such it is probably linked with the alternative form of the rune Jera or Ger, which represents the cycles of manifestation around the cosmic axis.

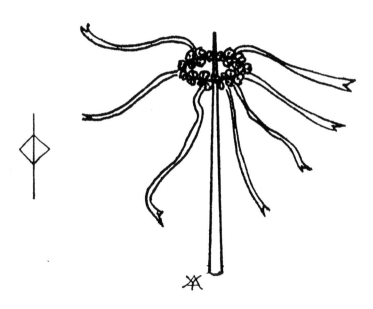

Alternative form of the
Rune Ger.

The maypole

Other runes representing the cosmic axis are: Algiz or Elhaz;Teiwaz or Tyr; Ior; Ear; and Gar (Odin's spear, the cosmic axis in microcosm).

In former times, every village in Germany had its own representation of the cosmic axis in the form of a linden tree with all but the top three branches removed: very similar in shape to the rune Algiz or Elhaz, which signifies protection.The purpose of the tree would have been both to offer magical protection and to give the village a symbolic centre.

A similar purpose is served by market crosses in England. Visit a town without one and you will notice the soullessness of it. Unfortunately modern planners do not take into consideration the geomantic aspects of town planning. This is extremely inconvenient for practitioners of magic, who generally find that their house is not precisely aligned in a northerly direction. This aside, the ancients appear to have known what they were doing when building towns, despite their lack of degrees in architecture etc. This is because they laid out the boundaries first, then divided the town into quarters, then built a cross in the centre (representing the four quarters of the earth), erected a pillar or a stone to mark the spot (and in the case of the Etruscans, dug a cavern beneath it to symbolise the underworld), and laid out the town according to their mental image of the cosmos. Of course, we all know that the earth is not flat, but psychologically we seem to need a centre and seven directions proceeding from it (within, above, below, north, east, south, and west). Otherwise we tend to suffer from a sense of dislocation and alienation.

Even nomadic tribes in Africa lay out their encampments like this (according to Mircea Eliade), the only difference being that the centre is a pole which they carry around with them, so that they are always at the centre of the world. Most nomads also follow a circuit, so that they are always in a particular place at a particular time of year, and can celebrate the festival associated with that time of year in the same place every year.

CHAPTER THREE:
TREES AND ALPHABETS

Veitstu, hvé rista skal? veitstu, hvé rada skal?
Veitstu, hvé fa skal? veitstu, hvé freista skal?
Veitstu, hvé bidja skal? veitstu, hvé blota skal?
Veitstu, hvé senda skal? veitstu, hvé soa skal?

Do you know how to cut and how to interpret?
Do you know how to paint and how to divine?
Do you know how to invoke and how to make offerings?
Do you know how to send and how to slaughter?

(The Havamal, stanza 144)

Closely related to cosmology, the association of alphabets and trees is very ancient. Oghams (and their close relatives, coelbren and the modern Irish alphabet) and Runes have tree correspondences which correlate with their symbolic meanings. An excellent book on this subject is Nigel Pennick's "The secret lore of Runes and other ancient alphabets".

Ogham

Legend has it that Ogham was discovered by Ogmios, the Celtic god of writing. Other cultures also attributed the discovery of writing to a deity, and restricted its use to a priestly caste, recognising its magical potential (by magical, I mean altering consciousness: the fact of being able to write things down which needed to be remembered has had a profound effect on mental processes). Similarly, the discovery of fire has been attributed to a deity by most cultures. Ogham was restricted originally to the Druids and the Bards; when its use became more widespread, they invented various coded forms of it.

Ogham

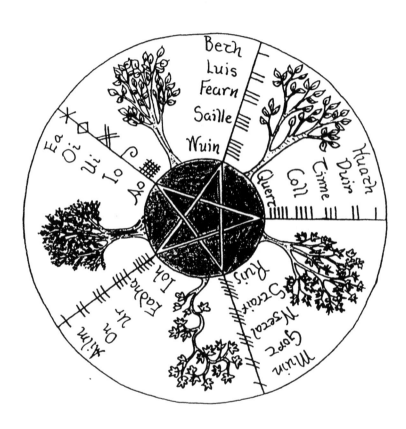

Coelbren

ᚲᚯᛟᚱᛚᚱᛖᚾ

ᛒ = Bedw
or
Beth

Coelbren (Welsh) after ɳ. Pennick   17-5-92

The Oghams are as follows:

Ogham	Meaning	Tree
Beth	Mother Goddess, purification, renewal	Birch
Luis	Flame; protection against psychic attack	Rowan
Fearn	Fire; blood; freeing earth from water	Alder
Saille	Linking; harmony; tides; moon	Willow
Nuin	Rebirth; linking upper and lower worlds	Ash
Huath	Hag aspect of Goddess; sexuality	Hawthorn
Duir	Door; midsummer; the god Taranis	Oak
Tinne	Fire; boldness; fatherhood; unification	Holly
Coll	Wisdom, divination, dowsing	Hazel
Quert	Eternity, rebirth	Apple
Muin	Gathering, assimilation, learning	Vine/Bramble
Gort	Scarcity, inadequate harvest	Ivy
Ngetal	Preservation; the written word	Reed
Straif	Strife, punishment, authority	Blackthorn
Ruis	Eternity; sacred to the Crone	Elder
Ailm	Rising above adversity; healing; foresight	Elm
Onn	Fertility	Gorse
Ur	Luck; freshness	Heather
Eadha	Preventer of death; resistance to change	Aspen
Ioh	Last day of the year; rebirth	Yew
Ea/Koad	Earth (Ea); the Eight Festivals (Koad)	Aspen
Oir	Childbirth	Spindle or Gooseberry
Ui/Phagos	Hardness; resistance; solid facts	Beech
Io/Pethbol	Mystery; the labyrinth; dance	Guelder rose
Ao/Xi/Mor	The pine: illumination (Ao) Spirit (Xi) The sea (Mor)	Pine or Witch hazel

It will be noticed how much of the symbolism of the trees concerned accords with their practical uses. Alder, for example, when immersed in water, becomes extremely hard, and is used to support buildings. It was also used for building roads across marshes. Hence the meaning of the Ogham Fearn, "freeing earth from water", i.e.

reclaiming waterlogged land. For similar examples, see the entries for the respective trees, under CRAFT USES.

Runes

The Runes have a less direct association with trees than the Ogham script, but nevertheless are associated with trees in magic and symbolism. The runic "alphabet" is called the Futhark, after the first six letters.

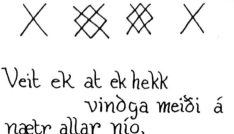

Veit ek at ek hekk
           vindga meiði á
nætr allar nío,
geiri undaðr ok gefinn Óðni,
sjálfr sjálfom mér,
á þeim meiði, er manngi veit
hvers hann af rótom renn.

I know that I hung
           on a windswept tree
for nine whole nights
wounded with a spear and
           given to Odin
myself to myself
on that tree, which no-one knows
from what roots it springs.

The Havamal, Stanza 138.

30

The correspondences are as follows:

Rune Germanic	Anglo-Saxon	Meaning / symbolism	Tree(s)
		FREYR & FREYJA'S AETT	
Fehu	Feoh	The primal cow; property; good name	Elder
Uruz	Ur	Horns of the ox; strength	Birch
Thurisaz	Thorn	Thorn; Thor's hammer; phallic power	Oak/Thorn
Ansuz	As	World Tree; knowledge	Ash
Raido	Rad	Cart; journey	Oak
Kano	Ken	Torch, illumination	Pine
Gebo	Gyfu	Sacerd mark; an exchange of gifts	Ash/Elm
Wunjo	Wyn	A wind vane; joy; glory	Ash
		HEIMDALL & MORDGUD'S AETT	
Hagalaz	Haegl	Hailstone; the beams of a house	Ash/Yew
Nauthiz	Nyd	Fire-bow; need-fire; catharsis	Beech/Rowan
Isa	Is	An icicle; steadfastness; standstill	Alder
Jera	Ger	The cycles of the year	Oak
Eihwaz	Eolh	Yew trunk; the underworld	Yew/Poplar
Perth	Peordh	The womb, birth; the mysteries	Beech/Aspen
Algiz	Elhaz	Elk; flying swan; splayed hand; sedge; protection; cosmic pillar	Service or Yew
Sowelu	Sigel	Rays of the sun; illumination	Juniper/Bay
		TYR & ZISU'S AETT	
Teiwaz	Tyr	Irmensul; justice	Oak
Berkana	Beorc	Birch; Earth Mother's breasts	Birch
Ehwaz	Eh	Horse; two poles bound; movement	Oak/Ash
Mannaz	Man	Human being	Holly
Laguz	Lagu	Leek; growth; a sea-wave	Osier
Inguz	Ing	Genitalia; fertility	Apple
Othila	Odal	Land; property; inheritance	Hawthorn
Dagaz	Daeg	Dawn; balance of night and day	Spruce

Additional
Anglo-Saxon Runes: AETT OF THE AESIR

Ac	Acorn; mark-tree	Oak
Os	Mouth; speech; a river-mouth	Ash
Yr	Yew bow; self-defence	Yew
Ior	Jörmungand, the world serpent	Linden/Ivy
Ear	Earth, the grave	Yew
Cweorth	Rising smoke; an offering	Bay/Beech
Calc	A drained chalice; chalk	Maple/Rowan
Stan	Stone; megalith	Blackthorn
Gar	Odin's spear Güngnir	Ash/Spindle

Additional Germanic Runes (not included in any Futhark)

Wolfsangel	Wolf-hook	Yew
Ziu	A lightning-bolt	Oak
Erda	Mother Earth	Elder/Birch
Ul	Turning point; Yule (Midwinter)	Sea Buckthorn
Sol	The Sun Goddess; the sun's disc	Juniper

Many correspondences can be found between the Runes and the Ogham script. Again, practical uses coincide with symbolism. In addition, the Runes are often pictograms of their symbolic meaning.

Tapestry Trees

Oak: I am the Roof-tree and the Keel:
      I bridge the seas for woe and weal.

Fir: High o'er the lordly oak I stand,
      And drive him on from land to land.

Ash: I heft my brother's iron bane;
      I shaft the spear and build the wain.

Yew: Dark down the windy dale I grow,
      The father of the fateful Bow.

Poplar: The war-shaft and the milking-bowl
           I make, and keep the hay-wain whole.

Olive: The King I bless; the lamps I trim;
           In my warm wave do fishes swim.

Apple-tree: I bowed my head to Adam's will;
               The cups of toiling men I fill.

Vine: I draw the blood from out the earth;
           I store the sun for winter mirth.

Orange-tree: Amidst the greenness of my night
                My odorous lamps hang round and bright.

Fig-tree: I who am little among trees
             In honey-making mate the bees.

Mulberry-tree: Love's lack hath dyed my berries red:
                  For Love's attire my leaves are shed.

Pear-tree: High o'er the mead-flowers' hidden feet
              I bear aloft my burden sweet.

Bay: Look on my leafy boughs, the Crown
           Of living song and dead renown.

(William Morris)

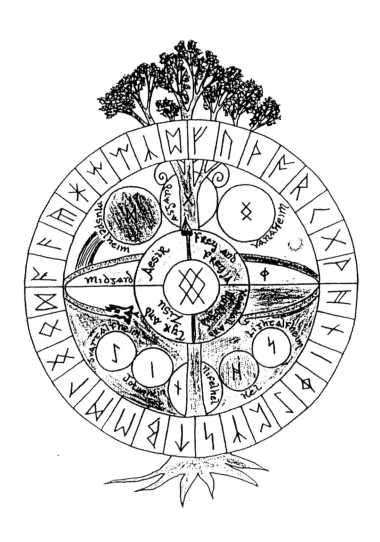

Northumbrian Futhark   30-6-92

34

CHAPTER FOUR:
TREE SPIRITS

Yet here, where never muse or god did haunt,
Still may some nameless power of Nature stray,
Pleased with the reedy stream's continual chant,
And purple pomp of these broad fields in May.

(from "Genius Loci", by Margaret L. Woods)

Many cultures have believed that trees have souls. As stated earlier, the initial stage of this belief is to ascribe an individual soul to each tree; later the culture may move on to the more sophisticated belief in a deity whose attribute is that tree (and who may have started out as a tree spirit) but who transcends the tree and may cover other aspects of existence. It is also possible to believe in tree spirits and larger deities at the same time. In Greek mythology, the nymphs of oak trees were called dryads; this term later appears to apply to all tree spirits. It is also possibly related to the word druid (derwydd in Welsh) meaning man of the oak, since both are probably derived from the same Indo-European root word. Caryatids (the unfortunate women found holding up temple roofs in Greek sculpture) were originally walnut-nymphs.

In India, a tree spirit was called a Yaksa. In Indian legend, it is related that when the Bodhisattva went to bathe in the river Nairanjana, he could not get back onto the bank without the help of a yaksa. In the Mahavamsa it is related that when Sakyamuni wished to go among the Nagas, where a war was imminent, he was accompanied on his journey by the yaksa of the tree Rajayatana in the garden Jatavana, which used its foliage as an umbrella to protect him. (The umbrella is one of the attributes of holy or royal personages in India.) Indian female tree nymphs were called Vrikshakas.

There is also the recurring image of the woman and tree in Prakrit and Sanskrit texts. It is known as the Salabhanjia: a pose of a woman pulling down the branch of a tree, carved in stone or wood. This does not represent a tree spirit as such, but the ancient custom (also found in Europe) of connecting the life of a person with the life of a tree.

In Buddhist art, the salabhanjia often represents Maya, the mother of Buddha, pulling down the branch of a Sala tree at Lumbini to induce labour, so that she might give birth to the Buddha.

In Jain temple art the salabhanjia is a preliminary object of worship, to focus the mind of the worshipper on the required qualities.

The earliest mention of salabhanjia was in the first century C.E. Thereafter it is widespread in Hindu, Buddhist, and Jain texts.

In modern India there is a children's game called coriya nuki (or in Bangladeshi, luko curi) in which several children chase a girl until she reaches a tree and touches its trunk, then bends down a branch. If she lets go they can 'take her prisoner' but if not she is 'protected' by the tree.

The image probably originated in the plucking of blossoms in springtime for making garlands and performing pujas (personal rituals of purification).

There is also the tradition of Dohada, the fertilisation of trees by pregnant women, which found its way into the Koran with the legend of Mary the mother of Christ sitting under a palm tree which Allah then made fertile, and thence into various songs and legends of Europe.

However, Dohada and salabhanjia may not be linked, as in salabhanjia the tree appears to be fertilising the woman, whereas in Dohada it is the other way round. Both however probably derive from an earlier tradition of tree-dwelling spirits (around the second or first centuries B.C.E.).

Further confusion arises in that salabhanjia is a classic pose in Indian art for depicting tree-goddesses, which may have served as models for the nativity pose of Queen Maya, the mother of Buddha. The pose consists of one arm bending down the branch, the opposite leg crooked round the trunk of the tree, and the other foot resting among the roots of the tree. Just to add to the confusion, the leg positioning appears to be borrowed from the Dohada posture. The salabhanjia pose is sometimes drawn with the woman sitting down.

Tree worship has been a part of religious experience since earliest times, when the earth was covered with primaeval forest, after the retreat of the last Ice Age. The origins of the Teutonic words for temple indicate that the earliest Germanic temples were woods and sacred groves. The ancient Slavs, Lithuanians, and Celts worshipped trees. The Lithuanians revered oaks and other great shady trees, from which they received oracular pronouncements.

Amongst North American Indians it is still believed that trees have spirits. To cut down a tree is regarded as unlucky without having first propitiated the spirit. It was the custom in many other places to apologise to a tree for cutting it down. However, in Jugra, in the Selangor region of Malaya, it was the custom to threaten to cut the durian tree down if it did not bear fruit. Threatening to cut down fruit trees which did not bear was also the custom in Bulgaria and other Slavic countries, and in Japan.

Ceremonies observed when cutting down a tree vary. It is generally agreed that propitiatory ceremonies must be performed, especially if the tree is haunted. Such rites include offerings of food; apologies; blaming it on the priest or the colonists (in Sumatra the Mandeling tribe used to blame the felling of a tree on the Dutch settlers); or leaving money at the foot of the tree. It is generally considered polite, if you are cutting bits off a tree for magical purposes (or any other purposes) to leave some kind of offering, or at least to ask the tree's permission.

In species where the male and female trees are two distinct plants, trees are often married to each other. The festivities of May are often celebrated with a Queen and King of the May; the May Queen is a living embodiment of a tree spirit, as is the Sacral King. If the King ailed, therefore, so would the corn, cattle, and people. Hence he must then be slain. In some cases he was slain at the end of a fixed term; in others he had to be killed by his successor, as the stag is displaced by a younger rival. The theory behind this was that if he could defend himself, his vitality and luck were still intact.

In ancient Harran the male pollen of the date palm was shaken over the flowers of the female tree, and the marriage of all the gods and goddesses was celebrated at this time, known as the date Month. On Christmas Eve German peasants used to tie fruit trees together with straw ropes to marry them and make them bear fruit.

In the Moluccas, clove trees are treated like pregnant women. When they are in blossom, no noise may be made near them, no light or fire may be carried past them at night, and hats must be removed in their presence, lest the tree should be alarmed and bear no fruit, or drop its fruit too soon, like a pregnant woman miscarrying.

Amongst the Dieri tribe of Central Australia, and some tribes of the Phillipines, trees are believed to be inhabited by the souls of the dead. They are said to prefer tall stately trees; when the wind rustles the leaves, it is said to be the voice of the spirit. When passing a tree inhabited by the spirit of an ancestor, it is customary to bow to it and apologise for disturbing the spirit's repose.

In China, trees are planted on graves to strengthen the soul of the deceased and save their body from corruption; evergreen cypress and pine are deemed to be fuller of vitality than most trees, hence are most often used for this purpose.

The people of Nias think that when a tree dies its spirit becomes a demon which can kill a coconut tree by lighting on its branches or kill all of the children in a house by perching on one of its pillars.

Tree spirits are also credited with beneficent powers. When a tree comes to be viewed as the abode of a spirit rather than as its body, this represents a move from animism to polytheism (according to Frazer). Ceasing to be a tree-soul, the spirit becomes the forest-god, the lord of the trees, possibly taking on human or semi-human shape. Beneficent powers of these gods include making the rain fall, the sun shine, flocks and herds to multiply, women to bring forth easily (this power is particularly ascribed to the maypole and the maytree in Europe), and making barren women pregnant (see salabhanjia above).

The primitive character of Osiris was as a tree spirit (as well as the man in the moon, who makes women pregnant, and the spirit of the corn). The body of Osiris was entombed in a tree; he was said to have taught men to train the vine to poles, to prune the superfluous foliage, and to extract the juice of the grape. Ivy was also sacred to him. There are some clear similarities to Dionysos here. Dionysos was particularly associated with fruit trees and the vine; the quince was referred to as the apple of Dionysos. He was also associated with the pine tree and the fig.

Another beneficial power of trees was to take on evils transferred to them. There are various folk customs associated with this.

In "Howard's End" by E. M. Forster, the locals used to stick pigs' teeth into the bark of the old wych-elm; chewing a piece of the bark was said to cure the toothache.

A Bulgarian cure for fever is to run three times round a willow-tree at sunrise, crying, "The fever shall shake thee, and the sun shall warm me." In Karpathos, an island of Greece, the priest ties a red thread round the neck of a sick person, and next morning the sufferer's friends go and tie the thread to a tree, to transfer the illness to the tree. In Italy the red thread is tied round the sufferer's left wrist at night, and transferred to the tree in the morning. A Flemish cure for the ague was to go early in the morning to an old willow, tie three knots in one of its branches, and say, "Good morrow, Old One, I give thee the cold; good morrow, Old One", and then turn and run away without looking round. In Sonnenberg, to rid one of the gout, they used to go to a young fir-tree, tie a knot in one of its twigs, and say, "God greet thee, noble fir. I bring thee my gout. Here I will tie a knot and bind my gout into it. In the name, etc." In some parts the custom for getting rid of gout was to place the fingernail parings and leg hairs of the sufferer into a hole bored in an oak tree, stop the hole up again, and smear it with cow dung. In Cheshire, to get rid of warts, they used to rub the warts with bacon, cut a slit in the bark of an ash, and place the bacon in the slit, the idea being that the warts would disappear from the hand and reappear as knobbly bits on the bark of the ash. At Berkhamsted in Hertfordshire, a lock of the ague-sufferer's hair was pegged into an oak, then the sufferer was wrenched away, leaving both hair and ague with the tree.

In England children were passed through clefts in ash-trees as a cure for rupture or rickets. Thereafter the life of the patient depends on the life of the tree, and if the tree is cut down, the rupture wil return and the patient will die. In some parts the method employed was to split a young ash sapling longitudinally and to pass the child three times through the fissure (often at sunrise), then to bind the cleft up again and plaster it over with mud and clay. As the tree healed, so would the child.

In many folk customs, a person replaced the spirit as the soul of the tree.

It was customary in Russia, Germany, England, France, and Italy to plant a tree at the birth of a child. In Switzerland, an apple tree was planted for a boy, and a pear tree for a girl. In Mecklenburg, the afterbirth was buried at the foot of a tree.

The earls of Dalhousie are associated with an oak called the Edgewell Tree, which grew near Edinburgh. In 1874 an old forester saw a branch drop from the tree, and exclaimed, "The laird's deid noo!" and sure enough Fox Maule, eleventh Earl of Dalhousie, had died that day.

In Indian folk-tales, the life of a man is often dependent on a tree because he has hidden his soul there for safe-keeping. This concept also occurs in the legend of Meleager, whose mother was told by the Fates that her son would die when the brand which was burning on the fire had burnt out. So she took the brand out of the fire and put it in a box. However, in after-years Meleager slew his brothers, so his mother burnt the brand, whereupon he died in agony as if flames were consuming him. Similarly, Balder's life was in the mistletoe (q.v.).

In Slavic folk-tales there is a forest-spirit, the Leshy. He had cheeks of bluish hue, because he had blue blood; tufty eyebrows, green eyes, often popping out of their sockets, and a long green beard. He had hair like a priest's, he wore his kaftan back-to-front and his left shoe on his right foot (a common practice of shamans, signifying the inversion of the normal order of things), and threw no shadow. When walking through the depths of the forest, his head reached the treetops; when he was on the edge of the forest, he turned into a tiny dwarf, and could hide under a leaf. He led people astray in the woods, making them go round and round in circles, but he usually let his victims go. To escape his enchantment, it was necessary to put all your clothes on back-to-front and your left shoe on your right foot.

The Leshy
(Polish
forest spirit)

The Leshy was not mortal but the offspring of a demon and a mortal woman. At the beginning of October, the Leshy would temporarily die. Revived in spring, he was then very dangerous and wild, full of anger and anguish. He would then wander the forest, whistling, shouting and cackling with laughter, sobbing and shrieking like birds and beasts of prey. Some legends give the Leshy a wife, the Leshachikha, and children, the Leshonki. All committed similar pranks to the Leshy. Each forest had its own Leshy.

It is hardly surprising that people should credit trees with having souls - they look so majestic, yet wild and free, and their lofty tops reach up into the heavens, whilst their roots probe the depths of the earth. They are so long-lived that it seems as if they must have acquired wisdom, yet they whisper it only amongst themselves when the wind stirs them. They have an air of mystery about them, and to penetrate into the depths of the forest truly mirrors the journey within, to the kingdom of the soul.

CONTACTING TREE SPIRITS

If you walk through a wood enough times, you begin to become aware of which trees are most powerful. Then, amongst these, you may find that one is the 'king-tree'. This is often an oak, but it may be another tree. The best way to contact the spirit of a tree is to start with one that you particularly like and build up a relationship with it. Stand or sit with your back to the trunk and exchange energies with the tree, trying to slow your consciousness to the rate at which the tree functions. Pagans believe that everything has consciousness, but not necessarily of a very complex nature. Trees are fairly complex, but being long-lived, they function at a slower rate than humans.

CHAPTER FIVE:
TREES AND THE WEATHER

Season of mists and mellow fruitfulness!
  Close bosom-friend of the maturing sun,
Conspiring with him how to load and bless
  With fruit the vines that round the thatch-eaves run;
To bend with apples the moss'd cottage-trees,
  And fill all fruit with ripeness to the core;
    To swell the gourd, and plump the hazel-shells,
  With a sweet kernel; to set budding more,
And still more, later flowers for the bees,
Until they think warm days will never cease,
  For Summer has o'erbrimmed their clammy cells.

  (from "To Autumn" , by John Keats)

Weather lore has many indicators in the natural world, the calendar and the hue of the sky. Among these natural indicators are trees.

When trees show the underside of their leaves, giving a lighter appearance than usual, it is a sure sign of wet weather. This phenomenon is most noticeable in poplar, lime, sycamore, and lilac.

If the wind makes a hollow sound among woodland or forest trees, it will rain. Before a dry spell, however, trees will snap or crack.

Few hips and haws on the trees indicate a hard winter to come.

A bumper crop of walnuts often coincided with the birth of many illegitimate children. In 1823 William Cobbett met an old man who said that "a great nut year was a great bastard year" and claimed that he could prove it from the parish records.

An old country saying has it that "When elder leaves are as big as a mouse's ear, women are in season". Similarly, "When gorse is in flower, kissing's in fashion".

The well-known rhyme about oak and ash gives a long-term guide to the weather:

  If the oak is out before the ash,

43

Then you'll only get a splash.
But if the ash beats the oak,
Then you can expect a soak.

I prefer the shorter version, which scans better:

Ash before oak,
We're in for a soak.
Oak before ash,
We're in for a splash.

The Shushwap Indians believed that they could bring on cold weather by burning the wood of a tree that had been struck by lightning. This belief may have been based on the observation that a cold spell often follows a thunderstorm in that region. Hence in spring, when travelling over the snow on high ground, they burnt splinters of wood from lightning-struck trees to prevent the crust of snow from melting.

Weathers

(i)

This is the weather the cuckoo likes,
   And so do I;
When showers betumble the chestnut spikes,
   And nestlings fly:
And the little brown nightingale bills his best,
And they sit outside at 'The Travellers' Rest',
And maids come forth sprig-muslin drest,
And citizens dream of the south and west
   And so do I.

(ii)

This is the weather the shepherd shuns,
   And so do I;
When beeches drip in browns and duns,
   And thresh, and ply;
And hill-hid tides throb, throe on throe,
And meadow rivulets overflow,

44

And drops on gate-bars hang in a row,
And rooks in families homeward go,
    And so do I.

(Thomas Hardy)

CHAPTER SIX:
TREES IN RITUAL MAGIC

Stand fast, root; bear well, top;
God send us a yowling sop!
Every twig, apple big,
Every bough, apple enow,
Hats full, caps full,
Fill quarter sacks full.

(Spell for a good harvest)

Trees have probably been used in magic since the discovery of agriculture made the vegetation spirit an important god. There are various magical uses of trees: divination, love spells, healing, protection, purification, etc.

Tree magic generally falls into the class of sympathetic magic, because it operates through the system of planetary correspondences, or the Doctrine of Signatures.

According to J. G. Frazer, sympathetic magic can be subdivided into two categories: homoeopathic magic (the law of similarity) and contagious magic (the law of contact). Homoeopathic magic is born of the idea that like begets like; if you perform an action on an object which represents something, the thing represented will be affected accordingly. Contagious magic is the use of a magically charged thing directly on the person or thing one is desirous of affecting; an obvious example here would be a talisman. Many forms of spell conflate the two types of magic.

Many people are sceptical of the existence of magic, but if, as some philosophers and physicists believe, reality can be affected by the observer, then a change in the consciousness of the observer will effect a change in reality. Hence Aleister Crowley's definition of magic: changing consciousness in conformity with Will (i.e. the higher self, the part of us which is godhead made manifest). The system of correspondences provides a framework and system for this change in consciousness to occur, invoking the archetypes associated with the desired effect. For example, the apple is ruled by Venus, so it is commonly used in love spells.

Trees are also used in magical rituals and burnt in the bonfire at festivals. The Nine Woods of the Beltane Fire are: ash, birch, yew, hazel, rowan, willow, pine, and thorn. Oak, however, should not be used, because it is the king of the woods. The woods burnt would probably vary according to local availability, but oak would not have been used, nor alder (sacred to Bran), nor elder (sacred to Hella, goddess of the Underworld).

The Yule Log, burnt at Yule, was traditionally made of ash. In some parts of the country, it was the custom for the innkeeper to burn one which was bound with three bands; whenever one of them snapped in the fire, a free round of drinks was served.

The seven Chieftain trees of old Irish law, which it was unlawful to fell because they were sacred, were hazel, apple, yew, holly, pine, ash and oak.

The word Rune comes from the same source as rowan. Related words include the Old English *rown*, to whisper, and the Gaelic *run*, a secret.

MAGICAL USES OF TREES

Protection

Trees which are used for protection are: ash, bay, buckthorn, coconut, cypress, elder, gorse, hawthorn, hickory, holly, ivy, larch, mistletoe, mulberry, oak, palm, pepper tree, plum, pomegranate, quince, rose, rowan, sandalwood, wild service, wayfaring tree, and witch-hazel.

Healing

Trees which are used in healing spells are: ash, aspen, bramble, horse chestnut, elder, eucalyptus, and lime (the fruit).

Invocation

Trees used for summoning spirits are: alder, bamboo, buckthorn, and yew.

Purification

Trees which are used in purification are: bay, birch, bramble, broom, cedar, gum arabic, lemon, osier, tamarisk, and willow.

Fertility

Trees used in fertility magic are: banana, birch, coconut, fig, mistletoe, oak, olive, orange, palm, pine, pomegranate, quince, and willow.

Divination

Trees used for divinatory magic are: apple, ash, hazel, orange, poplar, rowan, and witch-hazel. These can all be used for making Runes for use in divination (except perhaps orange and witch-hazel, which would be very difficult to obtain, and are not indigenous species).

Love

Trees used in love spells are: apple, apricot, avocado, brazil, cherry, sweet chestnut, lemon, papaya, plum, prickly ash, rose, walnut, and willow.

N.B. Love spells should only be used to encourage love, never to coerce someone into loving. For example, if two people obviously love each other but seem unable to communicate this, it is acceptable to give them a helping hand; likewise if a relationship is foundering due to lack of communication, a spell to facilitate this would be acceptable. Where the practitioner of magic is not a partner in the relationship, it is prudent to act only at the request of one or preferably both of the partners. If the practitioner of magic is a partner in the relationship, she or he should ask the other partner if he or she is willing. Some love spells involve finding out who your partner will be. This is inadvisable, since when you meet them your assumption that they will feel the same way may put them off altogether! It should also be noted that the karmic effects of coercive or inappropriate love spells last for seven years - the first six months are sheer hell, but the other six and a half years are not very nice either, so think VERY carefully before attempting any kind of love spell, even non-specific spells to attract a lover.

If you think you have been the victim of a love-spell, make use of the protective trees. The Arabs believe that eating pistachio nuts will break a love-spell, so try that as well.

Money

Trees used in spells for prosperity are: almond, horse chestnut, and gorse.

N.B. Spells for money or jobs should not specify the source of the money or job, since someone else may need that particular money or job more than you do. However, general prosperity spells are acceptable, provided they are not motivated by greed or laziness, but come from a genuine need. A proportion of any money gained by such spells should be given to another person, for such prosperity is a gift from the gods and should be shared.

The categories listed above are intended as a reference to refer the reader to the more detailed entries in the Tree Index.

PLANETARY RULERSHIPS

Incense makers, herbalists, and practitioners of magic may find the following list of planetary rulerships helpful:

Sun (principle of self-integration): balsam, bay, benzoin, cashew, cedar, citron, frankincense, grapefruit, gum arabic (acacia), hickory, juniper, hemlock tree, lime (fruit), mistletoe, olibanum, orange, palm, pine, spruce, thuja, walnut, witch-hazel.

Mercury (principle of communication): almond, ash, cassia, hazel, mace, mulberry, pecan, pistachio, pomegranate, rowan.

Venus (principle of unity, love, and friendship): apple, apricot, avocado, banana, birch, bramble, cananga, cherry, damson, elder, guelder rose, hornbeam, magnolia, peach, pear, persimmon, plum, rose, rosewood, spindle, wayfaring tree, whitebeam, ylang-ylang.

Mars (principle of action; phallic, warlike): dogwood, gorse, hawthorn, larch, pepper tree, prickly ash.

Moon (rhythmic principle: instinct, intuition, dreams): alder, aspen, bamboo, bergamot, broom, cassia, coconut, jasmine, lemon, linaloe, myrrh, olive, opoponax, osier, papaya, privet, sallow, sandalwood, willow.

Jupiter (principle of expansion, learning, and wisdom): banyan, blackthorn, bo tree, cajeput, sweet chestnut, horse chestnut, clove, fig, fir, lime or linden, field maple, great maple, niaouli, nutmeg, oak, plane, ti tree.

Saturn (principle of contraction, limitation, formation): beech, buckthorn, elm, eucalyptus, holly, ivy, mimosa, poplar, quince, tamarind, tamarisk, wild service, yew.

Pluto (principle of transformation through elimination and renewal): box, cypress.

Neptune (refining principle): ash.

Uranus (principle of deviation and invention): cedar.

Chiron (principle of healing: the Wounded Healer): ash, aspen, elder, eucalyptus.

When cutting fruit, leaves, boughs, twigs, nuts, etc. from trees it is customary to leave an offering to the spirit of the tree. Magic is said to work by the law of returns, that is, a gift requires a gift. Acceptable offerings include a vow of action, money, food, a libation, or at the very least, a prayer of thanks. (Vows could include promises to do something for the environment.)

In the case of money obtained by magical means, a portion of it should be spent on the poor and needy by the recipient, in order to share the benefit; otherwise the gods will not be so willing to grant your request the next time.

INCENSE

Smell is the most evocative of all the senses. Who has not stood among myrtle bushes on a hot day, and breathed in the pleasing scent; been reminded of their grandmother's house by the smell of new-baked bread; or had their senses uplifted by the subtle perfume of incense?

Many magical rituals require incense. In "The Sea Priestess" by Dion Fortune, the priestess kindles the Fire of Azrael, for insight into past lives. It consisted of juniper, sandalwood, and cedarwood. An incense can be made from these trees, using 1 oz sandalwood chips, 1 oz crushed juniper berries, and 10 drops essential oil of cedarwood, or, if you can get them, a green cedar cone (ground up small enough to burn), or some cedarwood chips.

50

Other ingredients of incense derived from trees are: willow bark, Gum Arabic (from the acacia tree), olibanum (from any tree of the genus Boswellia), oak bark, bay leaves, pine resin, cassia, bamboo, rose, jasmine, mistletoe, hemlock tree resin, ivy, rowan leaves and berries, opoponax, myrrh, frankincense, cassia, cinnamon, clove, nutmeg, mace, jasmine, balsam, ylang-ylang, lemon, lime, orange, rosewood, mastic, and cypress.

Cypress is burned as an incense to allay grief and to help heal invalids; the greenery from the tree can be dried and used as incense.For example, Cedar incense is used for purification and getting rid of bad dreams; Juniper incense is used by the Tibetans to expel demons; Mistletoe is burnt to ward off evil; Pine is used for purification; Rose petals are used in healing incenses; Rowan leaves and berries are added to divination incenses, along with bay leaves; and Gum Arabic is used for spirituality and purification.

TALISMANS

Talismans are a form of 'contagious magic', that is, they are charged magical objects carried on the person. Many people carry 'lucky charms' for stressful situations; these are a sort of 'mass-produced' talisman. Most talismans produced by a practitioner of magic, however, will be purpose-made for the occasion. If you are going to make your talisman from wood, it is a good idea to use an appropriate wood for the purpose, by referring to the lists of planetary correspondences and magical uses above, and to make an appropriate offering to the tree. The talisman is then carved with runes or planetary symbols (but not both - eclectic synthesis weakens the effect) and a phrase expressing the purpose for which the talisman is intended. Then the talisman is magically charged, invoking the appropriate deity.

MAGICAL TOOLS

Wands can be made of various different woods, according to their purpose. Divining rods are usually made of hazel, and hazel wands were used by the druids as a symbol of authority. A blackthorn staff can be used for authority also. Willow is used for any ritual associated with the Moon. Wands are often tipped with an acorn (symbol of fertility and renewal) or a pine cone (deal apple, symbol of Dionysos); the thyrsus of Dionysiac rites was a staff tipped with a pine cone. Again the lists of planetary correspondences and magical uses may be used as a guide.

The Celtic wand was made of hazel; the Gaelic white wand from yew. The wand is a conductor of power, used by witches, shamans, and magicians.

In many covens, the hilt of the sword was made of elder because judgement was traditionally given under elder trees. The witches' broom was traditionally made with a willow or hazel shaft, birch twigs for the besom, bound by thongs of ash or willow.

Wassail cups were traditionally made of maplin or maple wood. A recipe for the Wassail Bowl is given in the entry for MAPLE.

Sprite flails (for banishing malign spirits) are made of bramble, because of its qualities of psychic protection and binding.

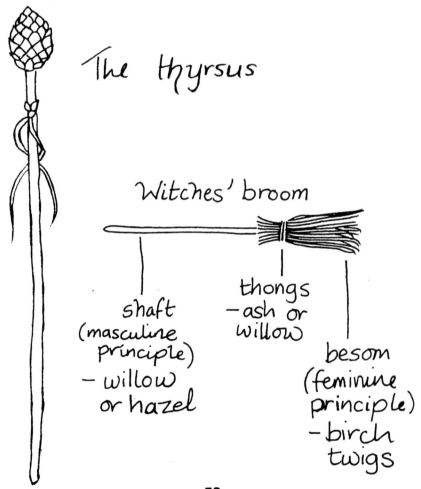

The thyrsus

Witches' broom

shaft
(masculine
principle)
– willow
or hazel

thongs
– ash or
willow

besom
(feminine
principle)
– birch
twigs

TREE INDEX

Acacia

LATIN NAME	Acacia spp.	POLARITY	Masculine
FAMILY	Leguminosae	ELEMENT	Air
FOLK NAME(S)	Cape Gum, Egyptian Thorn,	PLANET	Sun
	Gum Arabic Tree, Wattle.	DEITY	Osiris, Ra,
			Astarte, Diana

VARIETIES
About 800 species, including the wattle (A. armata); Mimosa (A. dealbata); A. longifolia; and A. pravissima.

MAGICAL USES
In India, it is placed in the turban to ward off evil. The wood is burnt in incense with sandalwood to enhance psychic powers.

SYMBOLISM
In Mediterranean countries it represents life, immortality, platonic love, and retirement. As having both white and red flowers, it denotes life and death, death and rebirth. Its thorns represent the horns of the crescent moon. The crown of thorns was said to have been made of acacia.

To the Egyptians it symbolised the sun, rebirth, immortality, initiation, and innocence. It was also an emblem of Neith, a sky-goddess and weaver of reality, whose earliest symbol was two crossed arrows on an animal skin.

To the Hebrews it was the Shittah Tree, the sacred wood of the Tabernacle, and symbolised immortality, a moral life, innocence, but also funerals and mourning.

The wattle (A. armata) is the national plant of Australia.

Alder

LATIN NAME	Alnus glutinosa	POLARITY	Feminine
FAMILY	Betulaceae	ELEMENT	Water
FOLK NAME(S)	Aller, Howler	PLANET	Moon
		DEITY	Bran, Pan, Verthandi
ETYMOLOGY	From OE alor, aler	RUNE	Isa
		OGHAM	Fearn

VARIETIES
30 known species. Grey Alder (A. incana); Italian Alder (A. cordata)

MAGICAL USES
For making whistles and flutes to summon spirits.In Ogham symbolism, Alder is quiet resistance. As the anima or inner woman, Alder 'bleeds' when felled, the wood turning from white to red.

MEDICINAL USES
Used to get rid of fleas; used as a poultice on burns and inflammations, and to refresh tired feet.

FOLKLORE
Alder trees should not be cut down.

SYMBOLISM
To the Celts, the alder was a faery tree of divination and resurrection, generally associated with death, the smith's fire, and the power of evaporation.

MYTHOLOGY
Alder trees are sacred to the Celtic god Bran, whose head gave oracular pronouncements after his death. In Greek mythology it was sacred to Pan, and the emblem of spring and fire festivals.

CRAFT USES
Used for piles to support buildings because it becomes very hard when immersed in water. Also used for clog soles, water barrel staves, weatherboards, and fine charcoal for gunpowder. The wood is knotted and easy to carve, hence it is used in cabinet making.

Almond

LATIN NAME	Prunus dulcis		POLARITY	Masculine
FAMILY	Rosaceae		ELEMENT	Air
			PLANET	Mercury
			DEITY	Attis, Mercury, Thoth, Hermes.

VARIETIES

Bitter almond (P. dulcis var. amara), containing benzaldehyde (95%) and cyanide (3%).

MAGICAL USES

Almond wood is often used to make wands. Climbing an almond tree is said to ensure success in business.

MYTHOLOGY

Nana, the mother of Attis, is said to have conceived by putting an almond in her bosom. In Phrygian mythology, it was the androgynous Cybele who gave birth to Attis,the almond springing from her genitalia.

SYMBOLISM

In Christian art, the almond symbolises virginity, the self-productive. The mandorla or vesica piscis is an almond-shaped halo often depicted as surrounding the Virgin Mary as Queen of Heaven.

As the first flower of the year, the blossom is the Awakener, hence represents watchfulness; it is also sweetness, charm, and delicacy.

In Chinese symbolism, it is feminine beauty, fortitude in sorrow, and watchfulness.

To the Hebrews, it is Skeked, 'to waken and to watch'.

In Christianity, it is divine favour and approval; and the purity of the Virgin.

In Iranian mythology it was the Tree of Heaven; to the Phrygians, the father of all things, Spring.

The almond is also associated with wisdom and hidden treasure.

Crab Apple

LATIN NAME	Malus sylvestris	POLARITY	Feminine
FAMILY	Rosaceae	ELEMENT	Water
FOLK NAME(S)	Crab tree	PLANET	Venus
ETYMOLOGY	From scrab (Scandinavian);	DEITY	Ing, Frey,
	a related word is 'crabbed',		Iduna, Pomona.
	meaning wrinkly.	RUNE	Ing
		OGHAM	Quert

VARIETIES

The crab apple is the parent tree of many orchard varieties; the apple is a close relative of the Whitebeam.

MAGICAL USES AND PRACTICES

Most magical uses are based on the domesticated species of the apple tree. Cider (from OE seidr, oracular divination) was used to induce altered states of consciousness. Anyone who has drunk scrumpy will no doubt agree that this does not take very long!

Apples are symbolic of the underworld, and as such are eaten at Samhain (Hallowe'en). Likewise, apple-bobbing at Hallowe'en is symbolic of the underworld and the subconscious.

When cut crosswise the apple displays two five-pointed stars - these are symbolic of women. In Cornwall, girls used to sleep with an apple under the pillow to ensure fertility and a good husband. Another apple love spell was to cut an apple in half and share it with one's lover to ensure happiness together. Offering an apple is a declaration of love, and apple blossom is used by brides. An European love divination spell was to cut an apple in two. If there is an even number of seeds, marriage would soon occur; if one seed were cut, it would be a stormy relationship; if two were cut, it would mean widowhood. However, if there were an uneven number of seeds in the apple, the querent would remain single for the near future.

Apples were also symbolic of fertility - cider libations were poured on freshly turned earth, or thirteen apple leaves buried after the harvest to ensure a good crop for the next year. Among the Kara-Kirghiz barren women would roll themselves on the ground under an apple tree to get offspring. At Beauce, near Orleans, the villagers make a straw figure called the great mondard , which is carried in solemn procession up and down the village and finally placed on the oldest apple tree. He remains there until the apples are picked, when he is taken down, burnt, and his ashes cast into water (the mondard represents the vegetation divinity). At Paturages in the province of Hainault (until about 1840) the villagers would run through the gardens and orchards throwing lighted torches at the fruit trees to encourage them to bear fruit.

In Aargau, Switzerland, an apple tree is planted at the birth of a boy (pear trees are planted for girls) and the child is supposed to dwindle or flourish with the tree.

In the Snow White story, the poisoned apple given by the queen has the red side dosed with poison (a homeopathic attempt to lessen the redness (vitality) of Snow White's cheeks. The queen eats the yellow half (the unattractive part) to "prove" that the apple is wholesome. In another version of the story, all of the apple is poisoned except the core, which the queen eats. This identifies her as queen of the underworld, giving death or radical transformation to those who eat the apple. Similarly, in the ballad of Thomas the Rhymer, the Faery Queen warns Thomas against eating any of the apples and pears in her garden, for to eat of the food of the dead means that there can be no return to the land of the living.

The nine glory twigs in the Anglo-Saxon Nine Herbs Charm appear to have been apple twigs:

"A snake came crawling, it bit a man.
Then Woden took nine glory twigs,
Smote the serpent so that it flew into nine parts.
There apple brought this to pass against poison,
That she never more would enter her house."

MEDICINAL USES

In the Bach flower remedies, the apple is used for purification and cleansing, for those who feel as if they had something not quite clean about themselves.

MYTHOLOGY

Avalon, the mythical isle of Glastonbury Tor, is said to have been an orchard (the Welsh for apple is afal). Unicorns are said to live under apple trees. Iduna, wife of Bragi (god of poetry) was keeper of the golden apples of immortality in Norse tradition. Apples were also the sacred food of the Celtic gods. Pomona was the Roman goddess of apples.

In Greek myth, the eleventh task of Hercules was to steal the Golden Apples of the Hesperides, which were watched over by the serpent Ladon. Similarly, in the Genesis myth of the Garden of Eden, the apple of the Tree of Knowledge is given to Eve by the serpent, and to Adam by Eve. The woman is the initiatrix. The serpent can be interpreted as representing 'dragon energy' (the energy of the earth) or Kundalini, the rush of energy up the spine experienced in meditation and spontaneous visionary experience. In Graeco-Roman orchards, a statue of Priapus was erected to protect the trees and make them fruitful.

SYMBOLISM

Apples can also symbolise treachery: in the myth of Atalanta's race, Atalanta was tricked into losing the race against Hippomenes by means of the apples which he threw into her path to distract her, thus winning the race, which enabled him to claim her hand in marriage.

In Christian symbolism, the apple is ambivalent; it can symbolise evil as the fruit of temptation and the Fall, but depicted with Christ or the Virgin Mary it is the new Adam and salvation. An ape with an apple in its mouth symbolises the Fall.

Apples were also used in Greek festivals. August 13th was a festival of Diana, at which a ritual meal was eaten, part of which consisted of apples still on the bough. In the Olympics, an apple-bough was awarded in the Sun-bridegroom race as a prize. (An olive-branch was awarded in the Moon-virgin race.) Apple-branches were also an attribute of Nemesis and Artemis.

In Chinese symbolism, the apple signifies peace and concord, whilst its blossom signifies peace and beauty.

RHYMES & SONGS

"Pear logs and apple logs
They will scent your room" (Dartmoor folk song)

"Here's to the old apple tree,
Whence thou mayest bud, and whence thou mayest
                    blow,
And whence thou mayest bear apples enow!
Hats full! Caps full!
Bushel, bushel sacks full!
Any my pockets full! Wassail!

(Wassailing song, accompanied by cider being poured over the roots of the tree, hitting it with sticks, and firing shots into the air. According to the Good Cider Guide, people would dip a piece of toast in cider to eat at the wassailing, leaving a piece in the branches for the robins. Wassailing generally occurred on January 5th or 17th. For wassail bowl recipe see MAPLE.)

"Apple-tree. I bowed my head to Adam's will;
The cups of toiling men I fill."
(from "Tapestry Trees" by William Morris)

CRAFT USES

The timber is fine-grained, suitable for turnery, cabinet-work, and engraving. Crab apples were sometimes used for making dolls' faces, which would 'age' very quickly, giving the doll the appearance of a very old person. The blossom can be used in perfumery.

CULINARY USES

Used to make crab-apple jelly and wine. The crab-apple was probably used for making cider before the advent of orchard varieties.

Apricot

LATIN NAME	Prunus armeniaca		POLARITY	Feminine
FAMILY	Rosaceae		ELEMENT	Water
			PLANET	Venus
			DEITY	Venus

VARIETIES

The genus Prunus has around 340 varieties, including peaches, almonds, cherries, and apricots (q.v.).

MAGICAL USES

Apricot pits are carried to attract love, and the juice is used in love spells and potions.

SYMBOLISM

As self-fertilising, the apricot symbolises the androgyne. In Chinese symbolism, it is death and timidity. .

Ash

LATIN NAME	Fraxinus excelsior	POLARITY	Masculine
FAMILY	Oleaceae	ELEMENT	Air
FOLK NAME	Heder (Lincolnshire)	PLANET	Mercury
ETYMOLOGY	Aes, a god (OE)	DEITY	Poseidon; Odin; Zeus; Jupiter.
		RUNE	Aesc/Ansuz, Os
		OGHAM	Nuin

VARIETIES

Flowering Ash (F. ornus); White Ash (F. americana)

MAGICAL USES

Divination and charms; Druids' wands; defeating ill-wishing; curing snakebite. Children suffering from rupture or rickets used to be passed through a split ash tree nine times. Thereafter the life of the child was dependant on the life of the tree; if the tree was cut down the rupture would return and the patient would die. It was also used to get rid of warts; in Cheshire, the custom was to rub the warts with bacon, cut a slit in the bark of an ash, and place the bacon in the slit. The warts were then supposed to disappear from the sufferer's hand, reappearing as knobbly bits on the ash's bark. In some parts the method employed was to split a young ash sapling longitudinally, then to pass the child three times through the fissure (often at sunrise), then to bind the cleft up again and plaster it over with mud or clay. As the tree healed, so would the child. Ash charms in the form of a solar cross were carried whilst at sea to prevent drowning (the ash is sacred to Poseidon, god of the sea). Ash leaves placed under the pillow are said to induce prophetic dreams; a garter made of the green bark was worn as a protection against sorcery. The first nail-parings of newborn babies were buried under ash trees to make them good singers. Ash leaves in a bowl of water by the bed were said to ward off illness (but the water must be replaced every night). Ash twigs placed in a circle were used as a charm against adders (perhaps a reminder of the serpent that gnaws at the foot of Yggdrasil - see MYTHOLOGY).

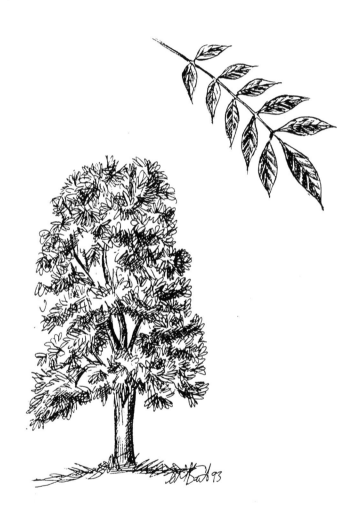

Ash

61

MEDICINAL USES

According to Culpeper, a distillation of the young tender leaves is good for dropsy and 'to abate the greatness of those that are too gross or fat'. A decoction of the leaves in white wine 'helpeth to break the stone and expel it, and cure the jaundice'. The ashes of the bark made into lye gets rid of scabs when applied to the head. The kernel found in the middle of the ash key is a diuretic.

FOLKLORE & WEATHER LORE

"Oak before ash, we're in for a splash;
Ash before oak, we're in for a soak."
(The rhyme refers to the appearance of leaves in spring.)

"Ash courts the flash" (country saying) - ash is prone to lightning strikes.

The ash is credited with great healing powers; snakes are said to shun even its shadow. It was considered very bad luck to cut down an ash without good reason. It is the last tree to come into leaf in the forest, so it stands for maturity and growing strength; adaptability, prudence, and modesty.

MYTHOLOGY

Odin hung on the world tree, Yggdrasil, a great ash tree, for nine days and nights. This shamanic ordeal yielded the discovery of the runes. The serpent Nidhogg gnawed at the roots, hence Ash is used as a charm against snakes. In Norse mythology, the first man, Askr, was made from an ash tree. Psychologically, the tree represents the animus. In Greek myth, it was sacred to Poseidon, Demeter's husband. It was also associated with the blood of Ouranos castration. The nymphs of the ash tree were the Meliae.

RHYMES & SONGS

"Ash logs, smooth and grey
Burn them green or old,
Buy up all that come your way -
Worth their weight in gold." (Dartmoor folk song)

"Even Ash, I do thee pluck,
Hoping thus to meet good luck.
If no good luck I get from thee,
I shall wish thee on the tree."

62

(To be recited when plucking an ash leaf with an even number of divisions on each side. Even Ash was traditionally worn in the hat or as a buttonhole.)

"Ash tree, ashen tree,
Pray buy this wart of me."
(Wart spell)

"If you find even ash, or four-leaved clover,
You will see your love afore the day's over."
(Even Ash)

"Ash. I heft my brother's iron bane;
I shaft the spear and build the wain."

(from "Tapestry Trees" by William Morris)

CRAFT USES

Fence posts; handles of tools and weapons; slats of coracles. Used by Scottish herdsmen for driving cattle. Broomstick handles were made of ash; also hockey-sticks, oars (another association with Poseidon?), carts, wheels, hop-poles, and furniture. Makes excellent fuel and charcoal.

Aspen

LATIN NAME	Populus tremula		POLARITY	Feminine
FAMILY	Salicaceae		ELEMENT	Water
ETYMOLOGY	From OE aespe		PLANET	Moon
			DEITY	Frigg
			RUNE	Perth
			OGHAM	Eadha

VARIETIES

American Aspen (P. tremuloides)

MAGICAL USES

Associated with the tarot card of the Fool, according to Aleister Crowley. Used for making magical shields. An aspen leaf placed under the tongue was said to ensure eloquence. Also used in anti-theft spells. In sympathetic magic, used for healing fevers and ague.

MEDICINAL USES

In the Bach flower remedies, Aspen is used for calming vague unknown fears which sufferers are afraid to tell to others.

FOLKLORE

According to legend, Christ's cross was made of aspen wood. Aspen is symbolic of the gifts of language and measurement; rulers are often made of aspen wood. Mete wands for measuring coffins were also made of aspen wood. The aspen is symbolic of fear, uncertainty, and lamentation.

RHYMES & SONGS

"Aspen tree, aspen tree, I pray thee
To shake and shiver instead of me."

(To be recited whilst pinning a lock of one's hair to the aspen's trunk; then one must return home in complete silence.)

CRAFT USES

Used for making matches, matchboxes, surgical splints, wagon-bottoms, floorboards, clogs, and pulp. It is virtually useless as fuel. The timber, once dried out, is light in weight and colour.

Avocado

LATIN NAME	Persea americana	POLARITY	Feminine
FAMILY		ELEMENT	Water
FOLK NAME(S)	Ahuacatl (Aztec: 'Testicle Tree'); Alligator Pear.	PLANET	Venus
ETYMOLOGY	from Spanish for advocate		

MAGICAL USES

Used by the Aztecs to induce lust. An avocado plant grown from the pit of the pear is said to bring love into the home; the wood can be used to make wands; and the pit is carried to enhance beauty.

MEDICINAL USES
Rich in vitamins A and B, as well as fat and protein.

CULINARY USES
The flesh is used to make guacamole, an excellent accompaniment for chilli con carne and other Mexican dishes.

Azalea

LATIN NAME	Rhododendron spp.	POLARITY	Feminine
FAMILY	Ericaceae	ELEMENT	Earth
		PLANET	Saturn

VARIETIES
R. albrechtii, R.arborescens, R. atlanticum, R. calendulaceum, R. flavum, R. indicum, R. kaempferi, R. kiusianum, R. luteum, R. nakaharai, R. obtusum, R. occidentale, R. quinquefolium, R. reticulatum, R. schlippenbachii, R. simsii, R. vaseyi, R. viscosum.

MYTHOLOGY
In Chinese legend, a tragic flower which grew from the tears of blood shed by a boy who was turned into a cuckoo by his cruel stepmother.

SYMBOLISM
Transitoriness; the ephemeral. To the Chinese, it symbolises feminine grace and great abilities.

BALSAMS

PLANET: Sun

Four separate species. all ruled by the sun

Canadian Balsam (abies balsamea) Pinaceae
Anti-septic (genito-urinary, pulmonary); astringent, diuretic, expectorant, purgative, regulatory, sedative, tonic. Useful for cystitis, coughs and colds, depression, stress, etc.

Copaiba Balsam (Copaifera officinalis) Leguminosae
Chronic cystitis and bronchitis - bactericidal, disinfectant, diuretic, expectorant, stimulant.

Peru Balsam (Myroxylon balsamum var. pereirae) Leguminosae
Anti-inflammatory, antiseptic, parasiticide, stimulant. Good for eczema, sores, wounds, nappy rash, rheumatism, low blood pressure.

Tolu Balsam (Myroxylon balsamum var. balsamum) Leguminosae
Expectorant, stimulant, antiseptic. Good for skin problems and respiratory tract infections. 1 teaspoonful in a steam bath is a good inhalant for catarrhal conditions.

Bamboo

LATIN NAME	Bambusa vulgaris	POLARITY	Feminine
FAMILY	Bambusidae, a subfamily	ELEMENT	Water
	of Graminae (grasses)	PLANET	Moon
FOLK NAME	Ohe (Hawaiian)	DEITY	Hina
ETYMOLOGY	Dutch bamboes, from		
	Portuguese mambu, from Malay.		

MAGICAL USES
Bamboo is considered lucky and a charm against evil spirits. Bamboo flutes are used to call up good spirits.

MYTHOLOGY

Hina was the lover of Te Tuna, the great sea monster, but she tired of him and sought a human lover. Only Maui dared to take her from Te Tuna. The story is retold by Richard Adams in his poem "Te Tuna". Hina is the goddess of the Moon in the Oceanic islands.

SYMBOLISM

Gracefulness, constancy, yielding but enduring strength, pliability, good breeding, lasting friendship; longevity and hardy old age (it is always green); the perfect man who bows before the storm to rise again. To the Chinese, it symbolises longevity, filial piety, and the winter season (with plum and pine, it is one of the Three Friends of Winter); it is an emblem of Buddha; and represents the scholar-gentleman who is upright in bearing but has an inner emptiness and humility. The seven-knotted bamboo represents the seven degrees of initiation and invocation. With the sparrow, it denotes friendship; with the crane, it denotes long life and happiness. To the Japanese, it symbolises devotion and truthfulness.

CRAFT USES

Furniture, flutes, and walking sticks are made from bamboo canes; the leaves can be used for matting.

CULINARY USES

The young shoots are used in Chinese cooking.

Banana

LATIN NAME	Musa sapientum	POLARITY	Feminine
FAMILY	Musaceae	ELEMENT	Water
FOLK NAME(S)	Maia (Hawaiian)	PLANET	Venus
ETYMOLOGY	Portuguese or Spanish, from a name in Guinea.	DEITY	Kanaloa

VARIETIES

All cultivated bananas are sterile hybrids, and are propagated from suckers arising from the underground rhizome. Wild bananas are small, brown, and rather unpleasant in taste. Larger varieties of banana, called plantains, are cooked as a staple food in East and West Africa and the Caribbean.

MAGICAL USES

Banana stalks are used as a substitute for humans in sacrifices in Hawaii and Tahiti; also the banana plant is used in voodoo rites to represent the gods, as it is hermaphroditic, bearing female flowers on the upper stem, which develop into seedless fruits without being fertilised, and male flowers on the lower stem, which hang down. The banana is used to increase fertility and cure impotency. It is considered lucky for brides to be married under a banana tree. Banana leaves, flowers, and fruits, are used in money spells. According to superstition, a banana should never be cut, only broken.

CULINARY USES

Bananas and plantains are very pleasant in curries and other hot dishes. Banana cake is also popular, and dried bananas are often eaten with muesli (which is much tastier made into porridge).

Banyan

LATIN NAME	Ficus benghalesis	POLARITY	Masculine
FAMILY	Moraceae	ELEMENT	Air
FOLK NAME(S)	Arched Fig, Indian Fig,	PLANET	Jupiter
	Indian God Tree,	DEITY	Maui
	Vada Tree.		(Hawaiian)
ETYMOLOGY	from Portuguese banian, from		
	Gujarati vaniyo, a man of		
	trading caste. The name was		
	applied to the tree because		
	some traders built a pagoda		
	underneath one.		

FOLKLORE

It is said to be good luck to sit beneath, look at, or be married under a banyan tree.

MYTHOLOGY

It is revered by the Hindus as sacred, and is often planted outside their temples. It is connected with the worship of Maui in Polynesia and Hawaii (see BAMBOO). Maui is an Oceanic folk hero, credited with the discovery of fire, creating islands, and even trying to obtain immortality for humanity. This last exploit, however, was the cause of his death.

PROPAGATION

The branches produce supporting aerial roots, which grow down to penetrate the soil and produce offshoots.

Baobab

LATIN NAME	Adamsonia digitata	POLARITY	Feminine
FAMILY	Bombacaceae	PLANET	Asteroid B612
ETYMOLOGY	Latin (1592), probably from an African language.		

CRAFT USES

The bark yields a fibre used in tropical Africa.

CULINARY USES

The flowers, which are pollinated by bats, develop into fruits containing a soft edible pulp surrounded by a tough woody capsule.

LITERARY ASSOCIATION

In "The Little Prince" by Antoine de Saint-Exupery, the soil of the planet from which the little Prince comes is infested with baobab seeds. Since the planet is only a small asteroid, baobab seedlings must be uprooted, or they will engulf the planet (asteroid B612).

Bay laurel

LATIN NAME	Laurus nobilis	POLARITY	Masculine
FAMILY	Lauraceae	ELEMENT	Fire
		PLANET	Sun
		DEITIES	Apollo,
ETYMOLOGY	Old French baie,		Aesculapius,
	from Latin baca, berry.		Ceres, Faunus,
			Eros.

VARIETIES
The cherry laurel (Prunus laurocerasus, family Rosaceae), spotted laurels (genus Aucuba, family Cornaceae), mountain laurel (Kalmia latifolia, family Ericaceae), and spurge laurel (Daphne laureola, family Thymeleaceae) are not related to the 'true laurel' or bay tree.

MAGICAL USES
The priestesses of Apollo chewed bay leaves and inhaled the fumes of burning laurel to induce a prophetic state. Bay leaves are placed under the pillow for prophetic dreams, and hung in the house as a protection against poltergeists, and in the window as a protection against lightning. A sprig of bay is used to sprinkle water in purification ceremonies. A bay leaf is held in the mouth to ward off bad luck. Bay twigs are broken in two by couples, who each take half to ensure the continuance of their love. Wishes are written on bay leaves, which are then burnt to make the wish come true.

MEDICINAL USES
In aromatherapy, essential oil of bay laurel is used for dyspepsia, flatulence, loss of appetite, dysmenorrhea, colds, 'flu, tonsillitis, and viral infections.

MYTHOLOGY
In Greek mythology, Daphne was a nymph transformed into a laurel tree by Gaea to escape from the unwelcome advances of Apollo. The laurel was thereafter sacred to Apollo.
    The festival of the Septeria commemorated Apollo's purification after killing the serpent Python. He went to the Vale of Tempe in Thessaly and returned to Delphi crowned with sacred laurel. The Septeria was celebrated every nine years. A youth chosen from the nobility represented Apollo. Accompanied by other young people he would set on fire a hut representing the serpent's lair. Then at the end of the festival the same youths would make a pilgrimage to the Vale of Tempe, practise

expiatory rites and return to Delphi with the sacred laurel. Laurel was also sacred to Artemis Agrotera, goddess of forests. When Hermes stole Apollo's heifers, he made a fire to cook them by rubbing twigs of laurel together.

SYMBOLISM

Made by Apollo into a symbol of honour and victory. Also a symbol of triumph; and as an evergreen, eternity and immortality. Consecrated to the Vestal Virgins, it indicated chastity. In Graeco-Roman symbolism it is victory, truce, and peace, and is sacred to Apollo, Dionysos, Juno, Diana, and Silvanus. In Christianity it is the crown of martyrdom. To the Greeks it was a crown for the victor or poet.

RHYMES AND SONGS

"Bay. Look on my leafy boughs, the Crown
Of living song and dead renown."

(from "Tapestry Trees" by William Morris)

CULINARY USES

Bay leaves are used to enhance the flavour of roast meats.

West Indian Bay

LATIN NAME   Pimenta racemosa
FAMILY   Myrtaceae
FOLK NAME   Bay Rum Tree

MEDICINAL USES

Essential oil of bay rum is used to stimulate the scalp, to get rid of dandruff, to promote hair growth, to combat greasy hair and enliven flat hair; and for aches and pains, rheumatism, sprains, colds, 'flu, and infectious diseases. Not to be confused with Bay Laurel (q.v.)

Beech

LATIN NAME	Fagus sylvaticus	POLARITY	Feminine
FAMILY	Fagaceae	ELEMENT	Fire
FOLK NAMES	Bok, Boke, Buche, Buk,	PLANET	Saturn
	Buke, Faggio, Fagos, Faya,	DEITY	Zeus
	Haya, Hetre.		
ETYMOLOGY	from OE bece	RUNE	Nauthiz
		OGHAM	Ui / Phagos

VARIETIES
Copper beech (F. s. 'Purpurea'); Cut-leaf or Fern-leaf beech (F. s. 'Heterophylla').

MAGICAL USES
The wood or leaves are carried to increase creative powers. A beech stick carved with the words of a wish is said to make the wish come true, if it is meant to be.

MEDICINAL USES
According to Culpeper, the leaves should be applied to swellings, and a poultice of leaves applied to scabs. In the Bach flower remedies, Beech is used for "those who feel the need to see more good and beauty in all that surrounds them" and to be more tolerant and understanding in general.

FOLKLORE
The Beech symbolises prosperity and divination; it is a tree of wisdom, and the emblem of Denmark. In Rhenish Prussia, on the first day of Lent, a Beech tree formed the central part of the Lenten fire. If the smoke blew over the cornfields, it was said that the harvest would be abundant.

'Pannage' was the custom of taking pigs to beech or oak woods to feed on beech mast or acorns.

MYTHOLOGY
In a tale related by Pliny, a Roman embraced, kissed, lay under, and libated wine to a beech tree in the Alban hills.

RHYMES & SONGS

"Beech-logs for winter-time."
(Dartmoor folk-song)

CRAFT USES

Plain furniture, tool-handles, and spoons etc. are made from beech. The bark is used for basket-work and band-boxes. In ancient times, the wood was used to make writing tablets.

CULINARY USES

The young leaves can be eaten as a salad ingredient. The kernels of beech mast are also edible.

Benzoin

LATIN NAME	Styrax benzoin	POLARITY	Masculine
FAMILY	Styraceae	ELEMENT	Air
FOLK NAMES	Ben, Benjamin, Friar's Balsam	PLANET	Sun

MAGICAL USES

Benzoin can be burnt alone or with other ingredients as a purification incense to clear an area of negativity.

MEDICINAL USES

In aromatherapy, benzoin is used for cuts, chapping, inflammation; gout, arthritis, rheumatism, poor circulation; 'flu, nervous tension, and stress. It can be inhaled via a steam bath to clear a blocked nose; this is even more effective when combined with eucalyptus (q.v.) and menthol oils.

Bergamot

LATIN NAME	Citrus bergamia	POLARITY	Masculine
FAMILY	Rutaceae	ELEMENT	Sun
ETYMOLOGY	from Bergamo in N. Italy	PLANET	Fire

VARIETIES
Bergamot is a dwarf variety of the Seville orange (C. aurantium). It is not to be confused with the herb bergamot (Mentha citrata), or another bergamot tree, a variety of fine pear, from the Turkish begarmudi, prince's pear (beg, prince; armudi, pear).

MEDICINAL USES
Essential oil of bergamot is good for clearing up skin infections and cystitis, and is used in cases of depression. It is a classic ingredient of eau-de-cologne.

CULINARY USES
The oil is used to give Earl Grey tea its distinctive flavour.

Birch

LATIN NAME	Betula pendula	POLARITY	Feminine
FAMILY	Betulaceae	ELEMENT	Earth/Water
FOLK NAMES	Silver birch, Beithe, Beth,	PLANET	Venus
	Berke, Lady of the Woods	DEITIES	Berchta, Frigga
ETYMOLOGY	from OE bierce or birce	RUNE	Berkana
		OGHAM	Beith

VARIETIES
Hairy birch (B. pubescens); Dwarf birch (B. nana); Paper-bark or Canoe birch (B. papyrifera); Sweet or Cherry birch (B. lenta).

MAGICAL USES
The twigs were used for flogging miscreants to drive out the evil spirit responsible for their crimes; bundles of twigs were given to couples on their wedding night to ensure fertility. May-poles were made of birch (another fertility association). In Russia it was the custom to tie a red ribbon round a birch tree to ward off the evil eye.

Stripped of its bark, the birch was burnt as the Yule log. Birch wood was also used to make babies' cradles (to provide magical protection, as well as for its association with birth, fertility, and springtime). Hence perhaps the French word for cradle, berceau, although the French for birch is bouleau.

Witches' brooms were traditionally made with willow or hazel for the shaft, and birch twigs for the besom, bound by thongs of ash.

The birch is the cosmic tree of shamanism, and the shaman ascends the seven or nine notches of the tree trunk or birch pole, symbolising the ascent through the planetary spheres to the Supreme Spirit.

MEDICINAL USES

According to Culpeper, the juice of the leaves is good to break up kidney- and gall-stones, and for washing sore mouths.

Oil from the bark can be used for skin conditions such as eczema, and birch tea, made from the leaves, used to be recommended for rheumatism and gout.

The buds are used as a tonic in hair preparations. Birch tar was used in folk medicine for eczema, psoriasis, etc. The sap tapped in spring was drunk as a tonic. The buds, leaves, and bark are used in rheumatism, arthritis, and urinary tract infections. The essential oil is used for dermatitis, the uses listed above, cellulitis, muscle pain, obesity, and oedema.

Sweet or cherry birch (B. lenta) is used in a decoction or syrup for dysentery and genito-urinary infections.

FOLKLORE

The birch is associated with rebirth, springtime, and fertility. The twigs are traditionally used to sweep saunas. The tree is the emblem of Estonia. In Russia at Whitsuntide, a birch tree is dressed in women's clothes and set up in the house. In Pinsk the girls of the village used to dress the prettiest of their number in birch and maple foliage and parade her about the village. At Misdsummer in Little Russia the women used to throw birchen boughs at a burning stake, saying, "May my flax grow as tall as this bough!"

The fly agaric mushroom (Amanita muscaria) is often found beneath birch trees. The presence of muscimol causes psychotropic poisoning, similar to alcoholic intoxication. It is not lethal but it can lead to coma in extreme cases. It was widely used as an intoxicant in Siberia before the introduction of alcohol to that region, and to induce shamanic visions. It is said to be Soma, the divine mushroom of immortality of early Eurasian religions.

MYTHOLOGY

According to Teutonic mythology, the last battle of the world will be fought round a birch tree.

RHYMES & SONGS

"Birch logs will burn too fast."
(Dartmoor folk song)

CRAFT USES

Oil extracted from the bark is used to dress leather. Birch twigs are used to make brooms. Canoe birch bark is used by North American Indians to make canoes. In Europe the bark is used for roofing and for tanning. Birch twigs retain their suppleness if soaked in salt water.

CULINARY USES

The sap of the tree is used to make birch wine and vinegar; the bark is used to make beer. The bark of sweet or cherry birch (B. lenta) is used by the North American Indians to make wintergreen and birch bark tea; these two plants are also used to flavour the American beverage root-beer.

Bodhi, Pipul, or Bo Tree

LATIN NAME	Ficus religiosa	POLARITY	Masculine
FAMILY	Moraceae	ELEMENT	Air
FOLK NAMES	Bogala (Sinhalese)	PLANET	Jupiter
		DEITIES	Vishnu,
ETYMOLOGY	Pipul, from Sanskrit		Buddha.
	pippala. Bogala = tree of		
	knowledge.		

MAGICAL USES

Meditation, attaining enlightenment; protection.

FOLKLORE

Both Vishnu and Buddha are said to have been born under a bodhi tree.

MYTHOLOGY
Sacred to Buddha as the tree under which he attained enlightenment. In India, revered as the source of Soma, the draught of immortality. When the New Moon falls on a Monday (Somavara), the women of Maharashtra dance round the sacred fig-tree in the rite of soma-vati.

SYMBOLISM
Perfection, contemplation, meditation.

Blackthorn

LATIN NAME	Prunus spinosa	POLARITY	Masculine
FAMILY	Rosaceae	ELEMENT	Fire/Earth
FOLK NAME(S)	Blackthorn, Sloe	PLANET	Jupiter
ETYMOLOGY	OE from Germanic	DEITY	Thor
		RUNE	Thorn/Thurisaz, Stan
		OGHAM	Straif

VARIETIES
Bullace (P. domesticus) is similar to blackthorn. Other close relatives are plums and damsons.

MAGICAL USES
Used as a staff of authority by witches, and in the Cochrane tradition, as a stang when cursing (see "Witchcraft: A Tradition Renewed" by Evan John Jones). Blackthorn thickets make good physical and hence also psychic barriers, and were used to ward off evil spirits.

Blackthorn or Sloe

MEDICINAL USES
Sloe gin is considered to have medicinal virtue.

WEATHER LORE
The tree usually blossoms when cold north-easterly winds blow, hence the country expression 'blackthorn winter', according to Gilbert White.

CRAFT USES
The wood is hard and tough, and takes a good polish, so it is extensively used for walking sticks.

CULINARY USES
The ripe berries can be made into a preserve, used to flavour and colour gin, or added to elderberry wine for a fuller flavour. (Elderberry and sloe wine is particularly potent and flavoursome made with burgundy yeast, available from all good wine yeast stockists.)

Borneo Camphor or Borneol

LATIN NAME   Dryobalanops aromatica

FAMILY   Dipterocarpaceae

MEDICINAL USES
This tree was known in Ancient Persia, India, and China; it was used against the plague, and stomach and bowel complaints. In China it was used in embalming. It repels insects and ants, so its timber was used in building.

It was mentioned by Marco Polo in the thirteenth century. In aromatherapy, its oil is used for cuts and bruises; as an insect repellent; for debility, poor circulation, rheumatism, sprains; bronchitis, coughs, colds, fever, 'flu; exhaustion, neuralgia, and stress.

Common Box

LATIN NAME	Buxus sempervirens	POLARITY	Masculine
FAMILY	Buxaceae	ELEMENT	Earth
		PLANET	Pluto
		DEITIES	Uller,
			Hades, Pluto
ETYMOLOGY	from Latin buxus, derived from Greek puxos		

VARIETIES

Buxaceae are mainly tropical, e.g. Balearic Box (B. balearica). There are seventy species (including garden varieties).

Box

MEDICINAL USES

A decoction of the leaves was believed to prevent premature baldness. Box is a purgative which raises body temperature. Not recommended for modern herbal use.

FOLK CUSTOMS

Sprigs and wreaths of box are often laid on graves and in former times sprigs of box were worn by the mourners at the funeral.

SYMBOLISM

Box symbolises immortality, youth, vigour, vitality and perpetuity (in common with many other evergreen plants).

CRAFT USES

The timber is very fine-grained, hard, and dense. It does not float on water. It takes a high polish, and was formerly used for engraving, carving, and small tool handles.

GARDEN USES

Box was very popular for formal gardens, both for hedges and topiary. Famous locations where box grows wild are Box Hill in Surrey, and the Devil's Dyke in East Anglia (referred to on the OS map as the Devil's Ditch, but known locally as the Devil's Dyke).

Bramble

LATIN NAME	Rubus fruticosa	POLARITY	Feminine
FAMILY	Rosaceae	ELEMENT	Water
FOLK NAME	Blackberry	PLANET	Venus
		DEITY	Dionysus
ETYMOLOGY	from OE braembel	RUNE	Thorn
		OGHAM	Muin

VARIETIES
Blackberry; the dog rose (Rosa canina).

MAGICAL USES
Used for making sprite flails, made from nine bramble branches an ell in length, well covered with thorns and bound at the base with willow bark collected in spring, to be used with the left hand (i.e., the banishing hand, so if you are left-handed, use your right hand). Also used for binding spells to contain energy (less destructive than using mirrors).

A bramble arch is used for healing, as follows: crawl through the arch backwards and then forwards three times, preferably from east to west. This is said to cure boils, rheumatism, whooping cough, and blackheads.

MEDICINAL USES
The leaves can be used to treat burns, scalds, and inflammations of the skin. Make them into a cold poultice. Blackberries are a good source of Vitamin C.

MYTHOLOGY
The thick growth of brambles in the Sleeping Beauty legend is the barbed tangle of the underworld which the hero must penetrate to attain the mystery. The castle is the soul, the hero is a man or his ego, the princess is the anima, and the brambles are his subconscious.

RHYMES & SONGS
The traditional charm against burns is as follows: float nine bramble leaves in a holy well, then draw them over the inflammation, saying:

"Three angels came from out the east,
One brought fire and two brought frost,

Out fire, and in frost,
Out fire, and in frost."

CULINARY USES
Bramble jelly; blackberry wine; blackberry and apple pie.

Brazil

LATIN NAME	Bertholletia excelsa	POLARITY	Masculine
FAMILY	Caesalpina	ELEMENT	Air
		PLANET	Mercury

MAGICAL USES
It is said to bring good luck in love affairs if it is carried as a talisman.

CULINARY USES
Used in cakes, biscuits, and as an ingredient of nut roast.

Broom

LATIN NAME	Cytisus scoparius	POLARITY	Masculine
FAMILY	Leguminosae	ELEMENT	Water
		PLANET	Moon
		DEITY	Bacchus,
ETYMOLOGY	from OE brom		Morpheus.

MAGICAL USES
The tough flexible branches were made into brooms, hence the name. Rhiannon Ryall states that she used a besom made of broom for sweeping the circle (West Country Wicca).

It is also used in purification and protection spells, especially against poltergeists (as an infusion sprinkled in the house). To raise winds, it was customary to throw broom in the air (preferably on a mountaintop) and invoke the spirits of air; to calm winds, one should burn broom and bury the ashes.

MEDICINAL USES

Thought to cure kidney and bladder complaints. It is a narcotic and a diuretic, but is NOT suitable for domestic use.

FOLKLORE

It is said to have been the plant which inspired the heraldic device of the medieval lords of Brittany and the Plantagenet rulers of England

SYMBOLISM

It represents humility and zeal in European folklore.

CRAFT USES

The tannin in the bark can be used to tan leather, and the flowers can be used for dyeing.

CULINARY USES

The young green tops were used to make beer bitter before the introduction of hops. Broom buds were pickled like capers. Not recommended for culinary use.

Buckthorn

LATIN NAME	Rhamnus spp.	POLARITY	Masculine
FAMILY	Rhamnaceae	ELEMENT	Water
FOLK NAME(S)	see Varieties	PLANET	Saturn
		DEITY	Waldh, Uller
ETYMOLOGY	Possibly OE buc, a male	RUNE	Ul
	deer, or ON bucca, a		(sea buckthorn)
	he-goat.		

VARIETIES

Alder buckthorn or berry-bearing alder (Frangula alnus); Mediterranean buckthorn (Rhamnus alaternus); and purging buckthorn (R. catharticus). Sea or Sallow buckthorn is not related, being of the Eleagnaceae family.

MAGICAL USES

According to Dioscorides, buckthorn branches placed near doors and windows will ward off enchantment and sorcery. Sprinkling buckthorn in a circle on full moon and dancing is said to make an elf appear. The dancer should say "Halt and grant my boon!" whereupon the elf will grant one wish before vanishing. Buckthorn is carried as a good luck talisman in legal matters.

MEDICINAL USES
The fruit, a black drupe, is extremely purgative, and the bark and berries are emetic, especially those of purging buckthorn (hence the name).

CRAFT USES
The bark yields a yellow dye, and the unripe fruits a green dye. The timber is still used in the manufacture of high-grade gunpowder.

Cacao

LATIN NAME	Theobroma cacao
ETYMOLOGY	Spanish from Nahuatl cacauatl (uatl = tree).

MEDICINAL USES
Taken in sufficient quantities, chocolate and cocoa are stimulant and psychotropic, containing the hormone phenylethylamine, which is very similar to the hormones produced by having sex.

CULINARY USES
Tree from whose seed-pods cocoa and chocolate are made.

Cajeput

LATIN NAME	Melaleuca cajeputi		
FAMILY	Myrtaceae		
		PLANET	Jupiter

VARIETIES
Cajeput is a close relative of the ti tree. It is also known as the white ti tree, white wood, swamp ti tree, and punk tree.

MEDICINAL USES
It is used in the East for colds, headaches, toothache, throat infections, aching muscles, fevers such as cholera, rheumatism, and skin diseases. Its uses in aromatherapy are similar to these.

Camphor

LATIN NAME	Cinnamomum camphora
FAMILY	LAURACEAE
FOLK NAME	Hon-sho

MEDICINAL USES
In folk medicine camphor is used as a preventative of infectious disease; a lump of camphor is worn on a string around the neck. It is also used in nervous and respiratory diseases. It is widely used as an insect repellent. It is poisonous in large doses, therefore used only cautiously and in small doses in aromatherapy. It can be used for arthritis, muscle pain, rheumatism, acne, inflammation, oily skin, bronchitis, chills, coughs, colds, fever, and 'flu. Rubbing your chest with camphor used to be a popular remedy for chest infections.

Cananga

LATIN NAME	Cananga odorata var. macrophylla		
FAMILY	Annonaceae		
		POLARITY	Feminine
		PLANET	Venus

VARIETIES
Cananga is a close relative of Ylang-ylang (C. odorata var. genuina).

MEDICINAL USES
In Asian folk medicine it is used for infectious illnesses such as malaria. Its flowers are used for decoration in folk festivals in Java, Malaya, the Phillipines, and the Moluccas. In aromatherapy it is used as an antiseptic, anti-depressant, sedative,aphrodisiac, and tonic. It does not have as subtle a perfume as ylang-ylang, but is nevertheless used in men's toiletries, soap, and perfumes.

Cascarilla

LATIN NAME   Croton eluteria
FAMILY   Euphorbiaceae

MEDICINAL USES

Native to the West Indies; its leaves are used as a digestive tea and for flavouring tobacco in the West Indies. The bark is used as an aromatic bitter. In West Indian folk medicine, the bark is used as a tonic for dyspepsia, diarrhoea, flatulence, dysentery, fever, debility, nausea, vomiting, and bronchitis. The aromatherapy oil derived from the bark is used for bronchitis, 'flu, coughs, dyspepsia, flatulence, and nausea.

Cashew

LATIN NAME   Anacardium occidentale
FAMILY   Anacardiaceae

POLARITY   Masculine
ELEMENT   Fire
PLANET   Sun

MAGICAL USES

Cashew nuts are used in prosperity and money spells.

Cassia

LATIN NAME   Cinnamomum cassia
FAMILY   Lauraceae

PLANET   Moon

MAGICAL USES

To the Chinese the cassia denotes immortality, a tree of life in Paradise, a tree in the moon, good fortune, and a rise to greatness.

MEDICINAL USES

The tree is found in China, India, and Vietnam, and is used in the folk medicine of these countries for dyspepsia, colic, diarrhoea, nausea, colds, rheumatism, and kidney and reproductive complaints. It has some pharmaceutical applications, but should not be used on the skin, and is therefore not used in aromatherapy.

Cedar

LATIN NAME	Cedrus libani	POLARITY	Masculine
FAMILY	Pinaceae	ELEMENT	Fire
FOLK NAME(S)	Cedar of Lebanon	PLANET	Sun
ETYMOLOGY	ME from Old French cedre from Latin cedrus from Greek kedros.	DEITY	Tammuz

VARIETIES
The deodar (Cedrus deodara) is a native of the Western Himalayas; and the Atlas Cedar (C. atlantica) is found in Algeria and Morocco.

MAGICAL USES
The incense is used for purification and to get rid of bad dreams. The wood is used in sweat lodges by North American Indians.

MEDICINAL USES
The essential oil of cedarwood is useful for a number of applications. However, Cedar of Lebanon is now very rare, so the red cedar (Juniperus virginiana, under Uranus) is now used instead. The Atlas cedar is also used, as is the yellow cedar (thuja occidentalis). The oil is good for cystitis and other infections of the genito-urinary tract; also catarrhal conditions, especially coughs and bronchitis. Externally, it is good for acne, oily skin, and dandruff. It is also a good insect repellent.

FOLKLORE
Said to have been used in the construction of Solomon's temple and palace at Jerusalem. Among the Kangra mountains of the Punjab, a girl used to be sacrificed annually to a cedar tree.

MYTHOLOGY
The Fire of Azrael in "The Sea Priestess" by Dion Fortune consisted of juniper, cedarwood, and sandalwood, and was said to induce visions.

In Assyro-Babylonian myth the forest, full of cedars, was the abode of the gods and

86

the sanctuary of Irnini, but also the dwelling-place of the monster Khumbaba.

SYMBOLISM
Emblem of Lebanon. Strength, nobility, incorruptibility. To the Christians, a symbol of Christ (Ezekiel 17:22), majesty, stateliness, and beauty. To the Sumerians, it was the cosmic tree, the tree of life; it possessed magical qualities and was sacred to Tammuz. To the Hebrews, it was a sacred tree.

RHYMES & SONGS
Mentioned in the Song of Songs in the Bible.

CRAFT USES
Used for chests, wardrobes, gates, seed boxes, and carved boxes. Valued for its scent, which repels insects, and is a pleasant fragrance.

Wild Cherry

LATIN NAME	Prunus avium	POLARITY	Feminine
FAMILY	Rosaceae	ELEMENT	Water
FOLK NAME(S)	Gean or Mazzard	PLANET	Venus
		DEITY	Venus, Aphrodite.
ETYMOLOGY	Cherry: from Old Norman French cherise from Latin ceresia. Mazzard: from mazer, a hardwood silver-mounted drinking bowl.		

VARIETIES
Sour cherry (P. cerasus), found in Asia Minor; bird cherry (P. padus).

MAGICAL USES
Used in a Japanese love spell: To find love, tie a strand of your hair to a blossoming cherry tree.

MEDICINAL USES
Culpeper's Herbal refers to the sour cherry (P. cerasus). He recommends it to "procure appetite to meat... to cut tough phlegm and gross humours." He also states

that "when they are dried... [they are] cooling in hot diseases and welcome to the stomach, and provoke urine: the gum of the cherry-tree dissolved in wine, is good for a cough, cold, and hoarseness of the throat..." The cherry is still used in modern cough remedies.

FOLKLORE

Cuckoos are often associated with cherries in folklore.

SYMBOLISM

As bearing flowers before leaves the cherry symbolises humanity born naked into the world without possessions, and as we also return to the earth. To the Chinese, cherry blossom signifies Spring, hope, youth, feminine beauty, virility, and the quality of Yin. In Japan, it symbolises prosperity and riches, and is a flower emblem of Japan. In Christianity, it is a fruit of Paradise, representing good works and sweetness, and is associated with the Christ Child.

RHYMES & SONGS

"Cherry logs across the dogs
Smell like flower of the broom" (Dartmoor folk song)

"Cherry-ripe, ripe, ripe I cry,
Full and fair ones, come and buy."
(Robert Herrick, 1591-1674: Hesperides, 'Cherry Ripe')

"There cherries grow, which none may buy
Till 'Cherry ripe' themselves do cry."
(Thomas Campion (1567-1620): Book of Airs)

"O ruddier than the cherry,
O sweeter than the berry,
O nymph more bright
Than moonshine night,
Like kidlings blithe and merry."
(John Gay (1685-1732): Acis and Galatea, II)

CRAFT USES

The yellowish to reddish-brown timber can be used for cabinet-making, furniture, turnery, pipes, musical instruments, and walking-sticks. Being flexible, cherry is an excellent wood for making quarter-staffs.

CULINARY USES

All domestic sweet cherries are descended from this species. The liqueur Maraschino is a strong sweet liqueur made from a small black Dalmatian cherry.

Cherry-ripe

Cherry-ripe, ripe, ripe, I cry,
Full and fair ones, come and buy.
If so be you ask me where
They do grow, I answer: There
Where my Julia's lips do smile;
There's the land, or cherry-isle,
Whose plantations fully show
All the year where cherries grow.
(Robert Herrick 1591-1674)

Song

There is a garden in her face
 Where roses and white lilies blow;
A heavenly paradise is that place
 Wherein all pleasant fruits do grow;
There cherries grow that none may buy
Till Cherry-Ripe themselves do cry.

Those cherries fairly do enclose
 Of orient pearls a double row
Which when her lovely laughter shows,
 They look like rose-buds filled with snow.
Yet them no peer nor prince may buy
Till Cherry-Ripe themselves do cry.

Her eyes like angels watch them still;
 Her brows like bended bows do stand,
Threat'ning with piercing frowns to kill
 All that approach with eye or hand
These sacred cherries to come nigh,
Till Cherry-Ripe themselves do cry!
(Thomas Campion, 1567-1620, Book of Airs)

Sweet Chestnut

LATIN NAME	Castanea sativa	POLARITY	Masculine
FAMILY	Fagaceae	ELEMENT	Earth/Fire
FOLK NAME	Spanish Chestnut	PLANET	Jupiter
		DEITIES	Tiw, Zeus, Jupiter.

ETYMOLOGY   from Old French chastaine, from Latin castanea, from Greek kastanea.

VARIETIES

There are ten known species in the north temperate zone, some rare.

Sweet Chestnut

MAGICAL USES

Used in love spells; the technique employed is to feed chestnuts to a loved one.

MEDICINAL USES

According to Culpeper, chestnuts thicken the blood. Taken internally, they stay bleeding and the coughing up of blood, and alleviate heavy menstrual flow. In the Bach flower remedies, sweet chestnut is taken for those moments of unbearable anguish, when it seems as if destruction and annihilation are at hand.

FOLKLORE

The chestnut tree is said to have been brought to Britain by the Romans. A chestnut tree grew on Mount Etna said to have been over 3000 years old, having a girth of nearly 50 metres. .

SYMBOLISM

In Christianity, it symbolises virtue, chastity, and victory over temptation, because of the thorny case surrounding the nut.

RHYMES & SONGS

"Birch logs will burn too fast,
Chestnut scarce at all;"
(Dartmoor folk song)

"The chestnut casts his flambeaux, and the flowers
Stream from the hawthorn on the wind away,
The doors clap to, the pane is blind with showers.
Pass me the can, lad; there's an end of May."

(A. E. Housman, 1859-1936, Last Poems)

"O chestnut-tree, great-rooted blossomer,
Are you the leaf, the blossom, or the bole?
O body swayed to music, O brightening glance,
How can we know the dancer from the dance?"
(W. B. Yeats (1865-1939), 'Among School Children')

CRAFT USES
Fence palings, posts, wine casks, walking sticks, coffins, and castanets.

CULINARY USES
Flour from chestnuts can be used to make bread. Roast chestnuts and chestnut stuffing are old winter favourites. In Majorca a dish called Imbuljuta is prepared from boiled chestnuts and chocolate sauce.

Cinnamon

LATIN NAME	Cinnamomum zeylanicum	POLARITY	Masculine
FAMILY	Lauraceae	ELEMENT	Fire
		PLANET	Sun
		DEITIES	Venus, Aphrodite

MAGICAL USES
Cinnamon was used in anointing oil by the ancient Hebrews; the leaves were woven into decorative wreaths in Roman temples. The Egyptians used cinnamon oil in mummification. Cinnamon is burned as an incense for spirituality, prosperity, psychic powers, and protection.

MEDICINAL USES
Cinnamon has been used for thousands of years in the East for colds, 'flu, digestive and menstrual problems, rheumatism, and kidney complaints, and as a stimulant. In aromatherapy, cinnamon leaf oil is used for the complaints listed above, and also for

hayfever, lice, scabies, teeth and gum care, warts, wasp stings, poor circulation, anorexia, colitis, diarrhoea, dyspepsia, chills, debility, exhaustion, stress, and to stimulate contractions in childbirth.

CULINARY USES
Used in tea, cigarettes, and as a spice in cakes and savoury dishes.

Citron

LATIN NAME	Citrus medica	POLARITY	Masculine
FAMILY	Rutaceae	ELEMENT	Air
		PLANET	Sun
ETYMOLOGY	from Latin		

VARIETIES
Related to lemon, lime, neroli, and bergamot etc. (q.v.), all members of the Rutaceae family.

MAGICAL USES
Eaten to increase psychic powers, and used in healing spells and incenses.

Clove

LATIN NAME	Syzygium aromaticum	POLARITY	Masculine
FAMILY	Myrtaceae	ELEMENT	Fire
		PLANET	Jupiter
ETYMOLOGY	from French clou, a nail (its shape resembles a nail)		

MAGICAL USES
Burned as an incense for purification and spirituality; or to stop gossip. It is worn or carried to attract the opposite sex, and to bring comfort to the bereaved. During plague epidemics, an orange stuck with cloves was carried to ward off infection.

MEDICINAL USES
In folk medicine, tincture of cloves is used for skin infections, toothache, indigestion, and childbirth pains. Clove tea relieves nausea. In Chinese medicine, oil of cloves

was used for diarrhoea, hernia, halitosis, and bronchitis, in addition to the uses listed above. Aromatherapists use clove bud oil, not the oil from the leaves or stem. It is used for acne, athlete's foot; as a mosquito repellent; for toothache, ulcers, wounds, arthritis, rheumatism, sprains, asthma, bronchitis, colic, dyspepsia, nausea, colds, and 'flu.

CULINARY USES
Used in tea, cigarettes, and as a spice in cakes and savoury dishes.

Coconut

LATIN NAME	Cocos nucifera		POLARITY	Feminine
FAMILY	Palmae		ELEMENT	Water
FOLK NAME	Sriphala		PLANET	Moon
			DEITY	Sri
				(Lakshmi)

MAGICAL USES
Used in spells for chastity and protection. A whole coconut can be hung in the home for protection, or one can be halved, drained of juice, filled with protective herbs, sealed shut, and buried to protect home or property.

MEDICINAL USES
Coconut butter is obtained from the lining of the coconut and used to make soap, candles, and ointment.

FOLKLORE
In northern India, the coconut is called Sriphala, the fruit of Sri, which is another name for Lakshmi, goddess of prosperity. It is a symbol of fertility, and is kept in shrines and presented to would-be mothers by the priests.

RHYMES & SONGS
"I've got a luvverly bunch of coconuts..."

CRAFT USES
Coconut matting is made from the husk of the coconut, which is called coir.

CULINARY USES

Creamed coconut is used in curries, particularly kormas, to obtain a lovely smooth sauce. Kormas were originally intended for the Brahmin caste.

Monterey Cypress

LATIN NAME	Cupressus macrocarpa	POLARITY	Feminine
FAMILY	Cupressaceae	ELEMENT	Earth
		PLANET	Pluto
		DEITIES	Hecate, Hades
ETYMOLOGY	ME from Old French cipres from Latin cypressus from Greek kuparissos	RUNE	Ear

VARIETIES

The Mexican cypress (C. lusitanica) was introduced to Britain at least three centuries ago, but is now rare. It was probably this tree that Shakespeare knew (see Rhymes and songs).

MAGICAL USES

Worn or carried to funerals, the cypress is said to allay grief. It is useful in times of transition or crisis. A cypress near the home is said to be protective, and the boughs are used in protective and blessing ceremonies. 'Healing stocks' are made from the cypress by slowly cutting, over a three month period, a wand from the tree, to be used solely for healing. This is passed over the afflicted person, touching the afflicted area, then its tip is plunged into the fire to cleanse it. The greenery can be dried and burnt as incense, especially in a room where someone is ill. A sprig of cypress is thrown into the grave to help the deceased in the hereafter.

MEDICINAL USES

Essential oil of cypress restrains discharge of fluids; it is antispasmodic, good for asthma, whooping cough, and all spasmodic coughs. It is also good for haemorrhoids, varicose veins, and oily skin. Culpeper says that the cones and nuts can be used to stop diarrhoea, incontinence, excessive menstruation, and bleeding.

FOLKLORE

The cypress has long been associated with death and mourning, due to its dark and sombre foliage. Its symbolism is equivalent to that of the yew. In Corfu, according to Gerald Durrell, they believe that one should not sleep beneath a cypress because the roots grow into one's brains and steal them, causing madness and loss of intelligence.

MYTHOLOGY

The ancient Minoans worshipped the cypress; and its wood was used to make coffins in ancient Egypt. In Greece, it was sacred to Hades.

SYMBOLISM

Tree of Death; funerary, mourning.

RHYMES & SONGS

"Come away, come away, death
And in sad cypress let me be laid"
(Shakespeare. Twelfth Night, II iv)

CRAFT USES

Stakes, vine props, carving, joinery, and furniture.

Damson

LATIN NAME	Prunus institia	POLARITY	Feminine
FAMILY	Rosaceae	ELEMENT	Water
		PLANET	Venus
		DEITY	Venus
ETYMOLOGY	ME damacene from Latin damascenus, meaning 'of Damascus'		

VARIETIES

Damsons are a subspecies of plum (P. domestica), generally smaller than the plum and often tapered at both ends.

MEDICINAL USES

According to Culpeper, dried damsons loosen the bowels and can be stewed to procure appetite and as a general tonic.

CULINARY USES

Damsons are grown for cooking and jam-making; they also produce excellent wine. Also used for making damson cheese, a solid preserve of damsons and sugar.

Date Palm

LATIN NAME	Phoenix dactilyfera	POLARITY	Masculine
FAMILY	Palmae	ELEMENT	Air
		PLANET	Sun
		DEITIES	Thoth, Ra, Apollo, Artemis, Ishtar, Isis

MAGICAL USES

Dates and pieces of palm leaf are carried to increase fertility; dates are eaten to increase fertility, and the pits are carried by men wishing to regain potency. A palm tree is said to protect its locality from bad weather, and a palm leaf at the door of the house is said to keep evil and uncanny creatures away.

MYTHOLOGY

In Greek myth, Apollo and Artemis were born to Leto under a palm tree. "Leto clasped a palm-tree in her arms, pressed the soft ground with her knees, and the earth beneath her smiled and the child leapt into the light." (From a Homeric hymn to Apollo.) In Egyptian ceremonial, Anubis marched in the procession in honour of Isis carrying palm fronds and the caduceus. In Egyptian myth, Thoth inscribed the happy years of rule accorded by Ra to the Pharaoh on a palm shoot, and the name of the heir to the throne on the sacred tree at Heliopolis.

SYMBOLISM

The palm is a solar tree, symbolising exultation, righteousness, fame, blessings, triumph, and victory. It is phallic, denoting virility and fertility, but depicted with dates, which symbolise breasts, it is feminine. To the Chinese, it represents retirement, dignity, and fecundity; in Christianity, it is the righteous "who shall flourish like a palm tree"; immortality if depicted with a phoenix; divine blessing; Christ's triumphal entry into Jerusalem; the martyr's triumph over death; and

Paradise. Palm branches signify glory, triumph, resurrection, and victory over death and sin; they were a funerary emblem among early Roman Christians, and an attribute of one who had made the pilgrimage to the Holy Land, hence the name 'Palmer'. It was also an emblem of St. Paul the Hermit and numerous martyrs. To the Egyptians it was the tree of the calendar, producing a branch each month (see also MYTHOLOGY). To the Greeks it was an emblem of Apollo; for the Hebrews it symbolised the righteous man, and Judaea after the Exodus. In Sumero-Semitic legend it was a Tree of Life, the emblem of the Phoenician Baal-Tamar, the Lord of the Palm, also of Astarte and the Assyro-Babylonian Ishtar.

Dogwood

LATIN NAME	Cornus sanguinea	POLARITY	Masculine
		ELEMENT	Fire
FAMILY	Cornaceae	PLANET	Mars
FOLK NAMES	Cornel, Bloody Twig,	DEITIES	Mars,
	Houndberry Tree, Catteridge		Ares, Teiwaz/Tiw
	Tree, Prick Wood, Widbin,		
ETYMOLOGY	Cornus = horny	RUNE	Teiwaz/Tyr

VARIETIES
Red osier dogwood (C. serica); Tartar dogwood (C. alba); and Cornelian cherry (C. mas).

MAGICAL USES
In parts of Russia a handkerchief soaked in the sap is used as a wishing symbol. In Slavonic countries its wood was sometimes used to kindle the needfire.

MEDICINAL USES
A lotion made from the bark is said to cure the mange in dogs, hence the name.

MYTHOLOGY
On the slope of the Palatine Hill there grew a cornel tree esteemed as one of the most sacred objects in Rome.

CRAFT USES
It was once used for making goads and dags (a dag is a spiked piece of wood used to drive animals). Also used for arrows, ramrods, mill-cogs, tool handles, toothpicks,

and skewers. It burns well and makes good charcoal for gunpowder. It is not surprising, then, that it is under the dominion of Mars.

Elder

LATIN NAME	Sambucus nigra	POLARITY	Feminine
FAMILY	Caprifoliaceae	ELEMENT	Water
FOLK NAMES	Lady Elder, Bourtree	PLANET	Venus
		DEITY	Hela
ETYMOLOGY	from OE ellaern	RUNE	Fehu/Feoh
		OGHAM	Ruis

VARIETIES
Red-berried Elder (S. racemosa); Blueberry Elder (S. coerulea).

MAGICAL USES
Elder twigs are woven into a head-dress at Beltane to enable the wearer to see spirits. Nine elder berries, or a twig cut into nine pieces, infused, is said by the Irish to be a cure for epilepsy. It is hung in front of stables to ward off malevolent sprites. Elderberry wine is used as a sacramental drink. Elder blossom is worn on Walpurgis Night, signifying witchcraft and magic. The elder is used to undo evil magic. It can also be used to bless a person, place or thing by scattering leaves and berries to the four wind, and over the person, place or thing being blessed. A cure for fever was to poke elder twigs into the ground, whilst keeping completely silent; a cure for toothache was to chew on an elder twig, and then poke it into a wall, saying "Depart thou evil spirit". Toothache was supposed to be caused by evil spirits, and spirits were supposed to have an affinity with elder trees. A cure for rheumatism was to tie a twig of elder into three or four knots and carry it in your pocket. A cure for warts was to rub them with a green elder twig and then to bury the twig in mud, the idea being that the warts would drop off as the twig rotted. Justice was often dispensed from under an elder tree, so the hilt of the coven sword was often made of elder. Flutes made from elder were used to summon spirits; and elder was used to make wands. Elder berries placed beneath the pillow are said to bestow peaceful sleep; and elder is carried to keep one from the temptation to commit adultery. Pregnant women kiss the tree for good fortune for the baby.

MEDICINAL USES
The leaves, crushed, are used for a poultice, and the flowers and fruit (rich in Vitamin C) can be used to make cough syrup. An infusion of the flowers is good for colds,

and Elderflower Water (Eau de Sureau) is good for the skin. The flowers are used in an ointment for burns, and the leaves in an ointment for bruises and sprains.

FOLKLORE

It is considered unlucky to burn elder wood or to bring it indoors. The wood should not be used as a switch for driving animals to market, nor to beat children, nor should it be used for cradles or poultry skewers. In Poland, it is customary to bury sins under an elder tree, where the tree's power would absorb them. Judas is said to have hanged himself from an elder tree. Amongst the Romanies, elder is known as Yakori bengeskro, or Devil's Eye, and it is forbidden to burn it.

MYTHOLOGY

Elder is associated with the underworld. In Germany it is called Hollunder or Hollerbusch, and it is sacred to the goddess Hela, queen of the dead, known to the Germans as Frau Ellen.

SYMBOLISM

The tree bleeds red sap when cut, so it is symbolic of menstruation.

RHYMES & SONGS

"Green elder-logs it is a crime
For any man to sell"
(Dartmoor folk song)

"Lady Ellhorn, give me of thy wood,
And I will give thee of mine
When I become a tree."

(Charm to be recited before felling an elder)

Neulich hab' ich gehext	Recently I conjured
DaB ein Höllerbusch wächst.	An elder bush to grow
Seine Blüten sind weiB,	Its blossoms are white
seine Beeren sind rot	Its berries are red
und sie bringen den Tod	And they bring death
daB weiB ich gewiB...	I know that for sure
komm pflück' mir und iB.	Come pluck me and eat

(German Elder song, 19th c.)

CRAFT USES
Tool handles, spoons, meat skewers (but not poultry - see FOLKLORE), whistles.

CULINARY USES
Elderflower champagne; elderflower fritters; elderberry wine; elderberry preserve.

Common, English, or Small-leaved Elm

LATIN NAME	Ulmus procera		POLARITY	Feminine
FAMILY	Ulmaceae		ELEMENT	Earth/Water
			PLANET	Saturn
			DEITY	Gefn
ETYMOLOGY	OE from Latin ulmus		RUNE	Gebo/Gyfu
			OGHAM	Ailm

VARIETIES
Wych or Scots Elm (Ulmus glabra);
Smooth-leaved Elm (U. minor);
Slippery Elm (U. fulva).

MAGICAL USES
Represents the death aspect of the
Earth Mother.

MEDICINAL USES
Bruised elm leaves applied as a poultice will heal septic wounds, according to Culpeper. In the Bach flower remedies, elm is used for periods of depression when one's chosen calling seems out of reach or impossible.

FOLKLORE
In "Howard's End" by E. M. Forster, the wych-elm at the bottom of the garden had pigs' teeth stuck in it, and chewing a piece of the bark was said to cure the toothache.

MYTHOLOGY
In Norse mythology, the first woman was Embla, an elm tree, and the first man Ask, an ash tree.

SYMBOLISM
In Christian symbolism the elm signifies dignity, and its great growth and spreading branches symbolise the strength and power of the scriptures for the faithful.

RHYMES & SONGS
"Elm-logs like to smouldering flax
No flame to be seen."
(Dartmoor folk song)

" .... at intervals,
The mythic oaks and elm-trees standing out
Self-poised upon their prodigy of shade"

(from "The Sweetness of England", by
Elizabeth Barrett Browning)

CRAFT USES
Elm wood is used for making coffins, furniture, parts of boats, bridges, piles, tool handles, wheelbarrows, panelling and cabinet work. In the past elm logs were hollowed out and used to pipe water.

Slippery Elm

LATIN NAME	Ulmus fulva		POLARITY	Feminine
FAMILY	Ulmaceae		PLANET	Saturn
			ELEMENT	Earth

MAGICAL USES
Slippery Elm is an American variety, and was used in American folk magic. It was burnt in the fire with a knotted yellow cord or thread to stop gossip and slander (yellow is the colour of Mercury, god of communication, and knotting is a binding magic); and the bark was worn about the neck by children to give them a persuasive tongue when grown.

Eucalyptus

LATIN NAME	Eucalyptus globulus	POLARITY	Feminine
FAMILY	Myrtaceae	ELEMENT	Water
FOLK NAMES	Blue Gum Tree, Stringy	PLANET	Moon
	Bark Tree		or Saturn

VARIETIES
There are 300 species of Eucalyptus.

MAGICAL USES
Used in healing spells and talismans, especially for colds. Its branches are hung over the sickbed. A healing spell involving eucalyptus is to ring a green candle with eucalyptus leaves and burn it all the way down, visualising the good health of the person.

MEDICINAL USES
The essential oil of Eucalyptus is used as a stimulant, and, diluted, as an antiseptic gargle. Locally applied, it reduces sensibility. It is good for spasmodic throat conditions, and is an expectorant and febrifuge. It is also good as a chest rub and an inhalant, as it is anti-catarrhal. It is also good for treating cystitis.

False Acacia or Locust Tree

LATIN NAME	Robinia pseudoacacia L.
FAMILY	Leguminosae
SUB FAMILY	Lotoidae

CRAFT USES
Formerly used to make the pins or trenails used to fasten the planks to a ship's ribs. The tree's seeds were imported to Europe from America in 1601.

CULINARY USES
An extract similar to licorice can be produced from its roots. Called the Locust Tree because early settlers in America named it after the Locust Bean in the Bible, which fed John the Baptist in the wilderness.

Fig

LATIN NAME	Ficus carica	POLARITY	Masculine
FAMILY	Moraceae	ELEMENT	Fire
FOLK NAME	asvattha (Sanskrit)	PLANET	Jupiter
ETYMOLOGY	ME from Old French figue	DEITIES	Juno, Isis,
	from Provencale fig[u]a		Dionysos,
	from Latin ficus.		Bacchus, Priapus,
			Jupiter and
			Silvanus.

VARIETIES
The fig is a member of the mulberry family, as are the bodhi tree (F. religiosa) and the banyan tree (F. benghalesis) and the mulberry tree (Morus nigra).

MAGICAL USES
Small phallic images carved from fig wood are carried by women wishing to conceive and men wishing to overcome impotency or infertility. Fresh figs are eaten for the same purpose. A fig tree grown in the kitchen is said to ensure that the family will never go hungry; and a fig branch placed over the door upon leaving is said to ensure a safe and happy homecoming.

MEDICINAL USES
Syrup of figs is both analgesic and purgatory (a cure for constipation). It is also said to be a good cure for a cough - you wouldn't dare cough once you had taken it. Mashed figs can be made into a poultice for boils, wounds, etc.; fresh juice from the leaves is said to cure warts.

FOLKLORE
It was a fig tree that Christ cursed for not bearing fruit; and Adam and Eve covered their genitalia with fig leaves (Genesis 3:2).

MYTHOLOGY
The fig is the cosmic or world tree in Vedic and Upanishad texts, having its root in the navel of the Supreme Being. "This everlasting fig-tree whose roots are in the air and its branches below, is the pure one, the Brahman, that which is called the undying. All the worlds rest on it, nothing happens outside it." (Katha Upanishad)

The sacred fig-tree of Romulus grew at Rome, and caused great consternation when it withered.

SYMBOLISM

"The fig-leaf is interpreted as denoting drinking and motion and is supposed to resemble the male sexual organ." (Plutarch) The fig symbolises fecundity, life, peace, and prosperity. The Tree of Knowledge in the Garden of Eden is sometimes represented as a fig tree. The leaves symbolise the lingam and the fruit the yoni. The fig-leaf depicts lust and sex. A basket of figs denotes fertility and the woman as goddess or mother. The fig is associated with the vine as a place of peace and quiet; and with the breast, as the 'tree of many breasts'. Both the fig and the vine were symbols of Israel, denoting peace, prosperity, and plenty. In Islam it is the Tree of Heaven, and sacred since Mohammed swore by it.

RHYMES AND SONGS

"Fig-tree. I who am little among trees
In honey-making mate the bees."

(from "Tapestry Trees" by William Morris)

Noble Fir

LATIN NAME	Abies procera		POLARITY	Masculine
FAMILY	Pinaceae		ELEMENT	Fire
FOLK NAME	Pitch-tree		PLANET	Jupiter
ETYMOLOGY	probably from Old Norse fyri		DEITIES	Pan; Woden
			RUNE	Kano/Ken

VARIETIES
Douglas Fir (Pseudotsuga menziesii)

MAGICAL USES
As incense, especially at Yule.

MEDICINAL USES
Culpeper describes pinus picea or the pitch-tree. The turpentine made from this tree is diuretic and good for wounds and ulcers.

FOLKLORE

Used in Germany to get rid of gout; one would go to the fir tree, tie a knot in one of its twigs, and say, "God greet thee, noble fir. I bring thee my gout. Here I will tie a knot and bind my gout into it. In the name, etc."

MYTHOLOGY

An early fetish of Osiris was the Djed, originally the trunk of a fir, but in classical times a pillar with four capitals.

SYMBOLISM

In Chinese symbolism, the fir denotes the Elect and patience.

RHYMES AND SONGS

"Fir. High o'er the lordly oak I stand,
And drive him on from land to land."

(from "Tapestry Trees" by William Morris)

CRAFT USES

Construction, joists, floors, interior joinery, and sounding boards for musical instruments

Frankincense

LATIN NAME	Boswellia carteri	POLARITY	Masculine
FAMILY	Burseraceae	ELEMENT	Fire
		PLANET	Sun
		DEITY	Ra, Baal
ETYMOLOGY	Frankincense means French incense		

VARIETIES

Frankincense comes under the general heading of Olibanum, which is a resin obtained from any tree of the genus Boswellia.

MAGICAL USES

Frankincense is used as an incense in China, India, and Europe. The ancient Egyptians burned it at sunrise in honour of Ra. It is burned for purification and uplift, exorcism, protection, consecration, inducing visions, and aiding meditation. It is added to sachets for good luck, protection, and spiritual growth. Inhaling oil of frankincense slows and deepens breathing, hence it is conducive to meditation.

MEDICINAL USES

It was used in folk medicine for syphilis, rheumatism, respiratory and urinary infections, skin diseases, and nervous complaints. It is used in aromatherapy for blemishes, dry skin, scars, wounds, wrinkles, asthma, bronchitis, catarrh, coughs, cystitis, dysmenorrhea, colds, 'flu, and stress.

FOLKLORE

Gold, frankincense, and myrrh were the gifts of the Three Kings or Magi to Christ. The gold represented his earthly kingship, the frankincense his spiritual kingship, and the myrrh his healing aspect as Christ the Physician.

COSMETIC USES

Used in ancient Egypt in cosmetics and perfumes.

Gorse

LATIN NAME	Ulex europaeus	POLARITY	Masculine
FAMILY	Leguminosae	ELEMENT	Fire
FOLK NAMES	Furze, Whin	PLANET	Mars
		DEITIES	Lugh, Jupiter,
ETYMOLOGY	from OE gors[t], from Old		Thor
	High German gersta	OGHAM	Onn

VARIETIES

Western Gorse (U. gallii); Dwarf Gorse (U. minor)

MAGICAL USES

Used for psychic protection; planted in hedges, especially in Wales. Also said to attract gold (hence sacred to Jupiter), so it is used in money spells.

MEDICINAL USES

In the Bach flower remedies, gorse is used for very great hopelessness and despair of finding relief.

FOLKLORE

"When gorse is in flower, kissing's in fashion."
(Country saying) This is because gorse is always in flower.

Gorse used to be grown extensively for fodder for cattle and horses. It burns well, even when green, because it is so dry.

Grapefruit

LATIN NAME	Citrus x paradisi	POLARITY	Masculine
FAMILY	Rutaceae	ELEMENT	Fire
FOLK NAME	The oil of grapefruit is also	PLANET	Sun
	known as Shaddock.		

VARIETIES

Member of Rutaceae family, which includes lemon, lime, citron, neroli, orange, and bergamot.

MEDICINAL USES

Oil of grapefruit is used in aromatherapy for acne, congested and oily skin, the promotion of hair growth, toning the skin, cellulitis, muscle fatigue, water retention, chills, colds, 'flu, depression, headaches, nervous exhaustion, and performance stress.

CULINARY USES

Used in savoury and sweet dishes.

Guaiac wood

LATIN NAME	Bulnesia sarmienti
FAMILY	Zygophyllaceae
FOLK NAMES	Champaca wood, 'palo santo'

The wood is used for ornamental carving. The aromatherapy oil is used for arthritis, gout, and rheumatoid arthritis.

Guelder Rose

LATIN NAME	Viburnum opulus	POLARITY	Feminine
FAMILY	Caprifoliaceae	ELEMENT	Water
FOLK NAMES	Cranberry Tree, Dog Rowan,	PLANET	Venus
	Water Elder, Dog Elder	DEITY	Arianrhod
ETYMOLOGY	from Dutch geldersch, from	OGHAM	Io/Pethbol
	Gelderland, a Dutch province		

VARIETIES
American Blackhaw (V. prunifolium); Nannyberry (V. lentago)

MAGICAL USES
The ogham Io or Pethbol symbolises the mysteries, the labyrinth, and the dance.

CULINARY USES
The ripe berries emit an offensive odour, but apparently in Siberia they are mixed with honey and flour to make an edible paste.

Common Hawthorn

LATIN NAME	Crataegus monogyna	POLARITY	Masculine
FAMILY	Rosaceae	ELEMENT	Earth
FOLK NAME	May	PLANET	Mars
ETYMOLOGY	OE from Germanic	DEITY	Thor
		RUNE	Thorn/Thurisaz
		OGHAM	Huath

VARIETIES
Midland Thorn (C. laevigata); Glastonbury Thorn (C. monogyna 'Praecox') - flowers at Winter Solstice.

MAGICAL USES
A hawthorn hedge affords good psychic protection. Glory twigs may have been made from hawthorn. It is said to cheer up the depressed if worn or carried.

Hawthorn

It is considered bad luck, however, to bring it indoors.

MEDICINAL USES
The powdered seeds dissolved in wine were used against gallstones and dropsy. Today, the flowers and berries are used in cardiac tonics.

FOLKLORE
Henry VII adopted hawthorn as his badge. Anne Boleyn is said to have married Henry VIII when the hawthorn was in flower and was executed at the same time the following year. It is considered unlucky to cut a hawthorn down; and sitting under one on May Day, Midsummer's Day, or Hallowe'en is said to result in being enchanted or fetched away by the faery folk, for the hawthorn is the meeting place of spirits and faeries. The tree is connected with various May Day customs; for example, in the Vosges mountains on the first Sunday in May, young girls go in bands from house to house, and if they are given money they pin a may bough to the house door.

WEATHER LORE

"Cast ne'er a clout
Till may is out."
(This probably refers to the hawthorn blossom rather than the month.)

MYTHOLOGY
Joseph of Arimathea is said to have gone to Glastonbury in 60 C.E. and stuck his hawthorn staff in the ground, where it grew and flowered - this is the origin of the Glastonbury Thorn.

SYMBOLISM
The blossom denotes virginity, chastity, or miraculous virgin conception. It was the Graeco-Roman bridal flower, sacred to Hymen, Chloris, Hecate, Flora, and the Roman Maia.

RHYMES & SONGS

"Hawthorn logs are good to last
Catch them in the fall."
(Dartmoor folk song)

"The fair maid who the first of May,
Goes to the fields at break of day,
And walks in dew from the hawthorn tree,
Will ever handsome be." (Beauty spell)

CRAFT USES

Tool handles, walking sticks, cabinet work. Burns well and slowly, giving off a lot of heat.

CULINARY USES

A liqueur can be made from the berries steeped in brandy.

Hazel

LATIN NAME	Coryllus avellana	POLARITY	Masculine
FAMILY	Betulaceae	ELEMENT	Water
FOLK NAME	Cobnut	PLANET	Mercury
ETYMOLOGY	Anglo-Saxon haesl, a staff of authority	DEITIES	Fionn, Thor
		OGHAM	Coll

VARIETIES

Turkish Hazel (C. colurna);
Filbert (C. maxima)

Hazel nuts

MAGICAL USES

Forked hazel twigs are used as divining rods, the straight stems for wands. Hazel was used by the druids as a symbol of authority, and by magicians to make ceremonial or magical shields. These were sacred to Fionn. Three hazel pins were driven into a house to protect it from fire; and hazel twigs were placed in window frames to protect the house from lightning (hazel is sacred to Thor).

MEDICINAL USES

According to Culpeper, the parted kernels made into an electuary (i.e. mixed with clarified honey) are good to help an old cough.

Hazel

FOLKLORE
Jacob used magic hazel twigs to produce mottled sheep and cattle in the Bible. The twigs were also used to kindle fires.

MYTHOLOGY
The pool of Connla, source of wisdom in Irish mythology, stood beneath a hazel tree whose nuts of inspiration fed the salmon in the pool. In Greek myth, hazel was the rod of Hermes, messenger of the gods, and hence symbolised communication and reconciliation.

SYMBOLISM
The nuts symbolise peace and lovers, hidden wisdom and the Mother Goddess.

RHYMES & SONGS

"To swell the gourd, and plump the hazel-shells
With a sweet kernel... "
(from "To Autumn", by John Keats)

CRAFT USES
Cask hoops, walking sticks, hurdles, thatching spars, etc. Not strong enough for structural use.

CULINARY USES
Hazel nuts are used in cakes, biscuits, etc.

Holly

LATIN NAME	Ilex aquifolium	POLARITY	Masculine
FAMILY	Aquifoliaceae	ELEMENT	Fire
FOLK NAMES	Hollin, Holm, Hulver,	PLANET	Saturn
	Helver, Poisonberry,	DEITIES	Saturn, Hodur
	Aunt Mary's Tree		
ETYMOLOGY	OE holegn; ME holin;	RUNE	Man/Mannaz
	modern English holly	OGHAM	Tinne

VARIETIES
There are 300 species in the genus Ilex, including I. paraguensis (see CULINARY

USES). The evergreen English holly has male and female flowers growing on separate trees; the female flowers develop into the red berries.

MAGICAL USES

Holly trees are planted outside the house, or their blossom is hung over the door, to ward off psychic attack lightning, poison, and evil spirits. It is carried by men for luck (ivy is carried by women), and was used to decorate druids' houses as a dwelling for tree spirits. Thrown at a wild animal, it is said to make it lie down quietly and leave you alone. Holly water is sprinkled on newborns for protection.

MEDICINAL USES

According to Culpeper, the fresh ripe berries are a purgative, whilst dried berries are good for preventing haemhorraging. This is NOT recommended, however, because the berries are poisonous. Edward Bach recommends Holly for easing thoughts of suspicion, jealousy, envy, revenge, or vexation which have no apparent cause.

FOLKLORE

Holly is sometimes depicted as the tree of the cross (as are Oak and Aspen).

MYTHOLOGY

Holly represents the King of the Waning Year, Saturn or Hodur. It was used in the Saturnalia as a symbol of health and happiness. (The Saturnalia lasted for seven days, from 17th to 23rd December. It involved an inversion of the accepted order; masters would serve slaves, and people gave gifts to all their friends.)

SYMBOLISM

Holly is a symbol of goodwill and joy; and an attribute of sun gods.

RHYMES & SONGS

"Holly logs will burn like wax
You may burn them green"
(Dartmoor folk song)

"The holly and the ivy
When they are both full grown
Of all the trees that are in the wood
The holly bears the crown."
(Christmas carol "The Holly and the Ivy")

Hollin, green hollin

Alone in greenwood must I roam,
   Hollin, green hollin,
A shade of green leaves is my home,
   Birk and green hollin.

Where nought is seen but boundless green,
   Hollin, green hollin,
And spots of far blue sky between,
   Birk and green hollin.

A weary head a pillow finds,
   Hollin, green hollin,
Where leaves fall green in summer winds,
   Birk and green hollin.

Enough for me, enough for me,
   Hollin, green hollin,
To live at large with liberty,
   Birk and green hollin.

(Anon.)

Birch: associated with fertility; used in the ceremony of beating the bounds.

Hollin / holly: associated with the festival of Saturnalia in ancient Italy.

Ogham months: Birch - December 24th to January 20th
                      Holly - July 8th to August 4th

115

"Then they sent men with holly clubs
To beat th' flesh from th' bones"
(John Barleycorn)

CRAFT USES

Turnery and marquetry; printing blocks; chessmen. Door handles and sills can be made from holly to enhance psychic protection. It is also used to make walking sticks.

CULINARY USES

Leaves of Ilex paraguensis are roasted, powdered, and infused with water to make mate, a stimulating tea-like beverage. I. paraguensis is native to Paraguay and Brazil.

Hornbeam

LATIN NAME	Carpinus betulus	POLARITY	Feminine
FAMILY	Betulaceae	ELEMENT	Air
		PLANET	Venus

MEDICINAL USES

In the Bach flower remedies, hornbeam is used for those who feel that they have insufficient mental or physical strength to cope with life.

CRAFT USES

Mill wheel cogs, rollers, and cattle yokes; chopping blocks, skittles, and piano parts. Very hard, tough and close-grained timber; makes good fuel.

White or Common Horse Chestnut

LATIN NAME	Aesculus hippocastanum	POLARITY	Masculine
FAMILY	Hippocastanaceae	ELEMENT	Fire
FOLK NAMES	Buckeye, Conkers	PLANET	Jupiter
ETYMOLOGY	see Sweet Chestnut	DEITIES	Tiw, Zeus, Jupiter.

VARIETIES

Red Horse Chestnut (A. x carnea Hayne); plus 25 other species from N. America, S. Europe,the Himalayas, China, and Japan.

MAGICAL USES

Chestnuts are carried to ward off backache, arthritis, and chills. Three nuts are carried to ward off giddiness. It is also carried for money and success, being under the dominion of Jupiter.

MEDICINAL USES

The red chestnut (A. carnea) is used in the Bach flower remedies for those who find it difficult not to be anxious for other people, but often have ceased to worry about themselves. The white chestnut was recommended by Bach for "those who cannot prevent thoughts, ideas, arguments which they do not desire from entering their minds [which will] cause mental torture... and interferes with being able to think only of the work or pleasure of the day." The bud of the white chestnut was recommended by Bach for "those who do not take full advantage of observation and experience", thus constantly repeating errors.

FOLKLORE

It is said that conkers were fed to broken-winded horses in Asia Minor, hence the name 'horse chestnut'. However, the fruits are poisonous to humans. Conkers, a game beloved of small children, involves threading the fruit on a string and hitting your opponent's conker until it smashes. A conker which has survived 99 such contests is called a ninety-niner.

CRAFT USES

Decayed conkers can be used as washing soap, as they contain tannins and saponins.

HISTORY
The tree is native to the Balkans, and was introduced to Britain in the sixteenth century.

Ivy

Horse Chestnut

LATIN NAME	Hedera helix	POLARITY	Feminine
FAMILY	Arialaceae	ELEMENT	Water
		PLANET	Saturn
		DEITIES	Osiris, Dionysos
			Bacchus,
ETYMOLOGY	from OE ifig	RUNE	Ior
		OGHAM	Gort

VARIETIES
Persian Ivy (H. colchica)

MAGICAL USES
Protection against psychic attack; carried by women for good luck (holly is carried by men). Used in fidelity and love charms.

MEDICINAL USES
According to Culpeper, the leaves steeped in rosewater and applied to the temples alleviate long-standing headaches; and steeped in vinegar and applied to the sides, will relieve aches, spleen, and cramps; this mixture is also bandaged to corns to relieve them.

FOLKLORE
The Flamen Dialis (the priest of Rome) was not allowed to touch or mention ivy, a goat, a dog, raw meat, or beans, amongst other taboos and prohibitions.

Ivy bushes were hung over the doors of taverns in honour of Bacchus, god of wine.

MYTHOLOGY
The Bacchanals ate ivy; it is believed to have been the cause of their divine fury. The eunuch priests of Attis were tattooed with a pattern of ivy leaves; ivy was sacred to Attis. In Egypt it was sacred to Osiris because it is an evergreen; it was also associated with Dionysos. Wreaths of ivy were worn as chaplets in honour of

Bacchus, and with the intention of preventing intoxication and hangovers.

SYMBOLISM

Jormungand, the World Serpent; Nidhogg, the dragon gnawing at the roots of Yggdrasil; death and rebirth mysteries.It also symbolises immortality, eternal life; revelry; clinging dependence; attachment, constant affection, and friendship. In Christianity, it symbolises everlasting life, death and immortality, and fidelity. The Hebrew name Rebekah means ivy, and signifies fidelity. To the Egyptians it was a plant of Osiris and immortality. In Greek myth it was sacred to Dionysos, who is crowned with an ivy wreath and carries an ivy cup; his thyrsus is entwined with ivy, and one of his symbols is a pillar entwined with ivy. Ivy was also sacred to the Phrygian Attis. The ivy leaf is phallic, and depicts the male trinity. Greek and Roman warriors adorned their armour with ivy, and poets were crowned with wreaths of it.

RHYMES & SONGS

The Tree-Entwining Ivy

I will pluck the tree-entwining ivy,
As Mary plucked with her one hand,
As the King of Life has ordained,
To put milk in udder and gland,
With speckled fair female calves,
As was spoken in the prophecy,
On this foundation for a year and a day,
Through the bosom of the God of Life,
and all the powers.
(Anon.)

"The holly and the ivy"

CRAFT USES

Thin slivers of ivy wood were once used as sieves, and the roots were used for sharpening knives. According to Izaak Walton in "The Compleat Angler", the resin from the broken woody stems of ivy makes bait more attractive to fish.

Common White Jasmine

LATIN NAME	Jasminum officinale	POLARITY	Feminine
FAMILY	Oleaceae	ELEMENT	Water
FOLK NAMES	Jessamin, Jessamine	PLANET	Moon/Saturn
ETYMOLOGY	from French jasmin, jessemin, from Arabic yas[a]min, from Persian yasamin		

VARIETIES
Primrose Jasmine (J. primulinum) from China; Winter-flowering Jasmine (J. nudiflorum) from China; Himalayan Jasmine (J. revolutum) from the Himalayas and Afghanistan); and J. polyanthum from China.

Jasminum officinale

MAGICAL USES
It is used to attract spiritual love; to induce prophetic dreams; and inhaled, to induce sleep.

MEDICINAL USES
Essential oil of jasmine is used in aromatherapy for dry. greasy, irritated, or sensitive skin; muscular spasms, sprains, catarrh, coughs, hoarseness, laryngitis; dysmenorrhea, labour pains; depression, nervous exhaustion, stress.

CULINARY USES
Jasmine flowers are used to impart the delicate flavour of Jasmine tea, which is excellent for cleansing the palate.

Juniper

LATIN NAME	Juniperus communis	POLARITY	Masculine
FAMILY	Cupressaceae	ELEMENT	Air/Fire
FOLK NAMES	Geneva, Gin Berry, Gin Plant	PLANET	Sun
		DEITIES	Balder, Hermes, Mercury
ETYMOLOGY	ME from Latin	RUNE	Sigel/Sowelu

VARIETIES
Dwarf Juniper (J. communis var. nana). Garden species: Chinese juniper (J. chinensis); pencil cedar (J. virginiana); creeping savin (J. sabina).

MAGICAL USES
In Scotland, juniper twigs were used for warding off the evil eye. Juniper incense is said to drive away demons, ghosts, and evil spirits, and to break hexes and curses. it is used as such by Mediterranean witches. The Tibetans also use juniper incense to expel demons.

MEDICINAL USES
Antidote to snakebite; berries are a good remedy for scurvy; oil of juniper dispels wind. It is used in modern medicine; an infusion of the berries is thought to be diuretic and good for cystitis. It also soothes aching muscles. It should not be taken during pregnancy or by people with kidney problems, however. Juniper oil was used as a panacea in the folk medicine of the former Yugoslavia. It makes a good bath oil, being both stimulating and relaxing; it is a diuretic, and useful against urinary tract infections. It is a good astringent and antiseptic, and is good for acne and dermatitis.

FOLKLORE
The foliage is used for kindling fires by country people. In Central Europe, juniper berries and rue were burnt in the house for the last three days in April as part of the general precautions against sorcery. The tree which sheltered the prophet Elijah when he was fleeing from Queen Jezebel was said to have been a juniper.

MYTHOLOGY
In "The Sea Priestess" by Dion Fortune, juniper, cedarwood, and sandalwood were used to kindle the Fire of Azrael, which was used for insight into past lives.

121

SYMBOLISM
In Graeco-Roman symbolism juniper signified protection, confidence, and initiative; it was sacred to Hermes and Mercury.

CRAFT USES
The wood was used for making dirk handles; it is aromatic and insect repellent, so it is used for cupboard linings; it is also used for making pencils.

CULINARY USES
Juniper berries can be used in soups, stews, and pickles to add flavour. The fruits are distilled to make oil of juniper; the crushed berries are added to marinades for game and stuffing for poultry. Juniper is also used to flavour gin and other spirits and beer.

Common Laburnum or Golden Rain

LATIN NAME	Laburnum anagyroides
FAMILY	Leguminosae

MEDICINAL USES
All parts of the plant are poisonous. Laburnum is mentioned in Gerard's Herbal (1597) - he had one in his garden.

CRAFT USES
The timber is used in cabinet-work, turnery,wood sculpture, and wind instruments. Furniture inlays are made from the end grain of the wood, known as 'oyster shell'.

Larch

LATIN NAME	Larix decidua	POLARITY	Masculine
FAMILY	Pinaceae	ELEMENT	Fire
ETYMOLOGY	Middle High German larche, ultimately from Latin larix or laricis	PLANET	Mars

VARIETIES
Larix decidua was introduced to Britain in the 17th century; Japanese Larch (L.

kaempferi) was introduced to Britain in 1861; and there is a hybrid of the two, the Dunkeld Larch.

MAGICAL USES

According to magical tradition, larch is impervious to fire, and it used as a charm for protection against fire. It is also carried or worn as a protection against sorcery and the evil eye.

MEDICINAL USES

In the Bach flower remedies, it is used for those who expect failure and consider themselves inferior to others.

CRAFT USES

The bark is used for tanning, and Venice turpentine is extracted from the trunk. The wood is used for fence posts, lap fencing, hop poles, rustic work, pit props, scaffolding, boat planking, and piling. It withstands alternating wet and dry conditions well.

Lemon

LATIN NAME	Citrus limon	POLARITY	Feminine
FAMILY	Rutaceae	ELEMENT	Moon
		PLANET	Water
		DEITY	Diana

VARIETIES

There are about 12 species in the genus Citrus, including oranges, lemons, limes, grapefruit, bitter orange, etc.

MAGICAL USES

Lemon juice mixed with water is used for cleansing amulets, jewellery, and magical items obtained second hand, removing any negative energy. Lemon juice can also be added to the purificatory bath at Full Moon. Lemons are believed to ensure fidelity and long-lasting friendship, hence lemon pie given to a loved one, or a lemon tree grown from the seed of a lemon that you have eaten, make good gifts. In "Aradia: Gospel of the Witches" there is a lemon spell; the lemon

Lemon

☽

123

should be plucked at Full Moon, with a conjuration of Diana, have pins stuck in it (but do not use black ones, as they are for cursing), and be given to a friend.

MEDICINAL USES

Lemons are rich in Vitamin C, and are used in hot toddy to soothe a sore throat. To make hot toddy, make fresh tea, add a tablespoonful of lemon juice, two fingers of whisky, and a tablespoonful of honey. In aromatherapy, lemon oil is used for acne, anaemia, brittle nails, boils, chilblains, corns, cuts, greasy skin, herpes, insect bites, mouth ulcers, spots, varicose veins, warts, arthritis, cellulitis, high blood pressure, nose-bleeds, obesity, poor circulation, rheumatism, asthma, throat infections, dyspepsia, colds, 'flu, and fever.

FOLKLORE

In India, ogres were said to keep their souls in lemons.

SYMBOLISM

Sourness; sharpness. In Christian symbolism it depicts faithfulness in love. In Hebrew symbolism it represents the harvest, and was carried in the left hand at the Feast of Tabernacles. It also appears to have some connection with the fir-cone in the rites of Dionysos.

RHYMES & SONGS

"Oranges and lemons
Say the bells of St. Clements"
(Nursery rhyme)

CULINARY USES

Lemon meringue pie.

Lime (fruit)

LATIN NAME	Citrus aurantifolia	POLARITY	Masculine
FAMILY	Rutaceae	ELEMENT	Fire
		PLANET	Sun
ETYMOLOGY	ultimately from Arabic lima, via Spanish, Provencal, and French		

VARIETIES
There are about 12 species in the genus Citrus,including limes, lemons, and oranges.

MAGICAL USES
A fresh lime pierced with iron nails, spikes, pins, and needles, and thrown into a deep hole in the ground is believed to rid one of all ills and hexes. A necklace of limes was worn as a cure for a sore throat. Nails were driven into the bark (having offered thanks to the tree) as a cure for toothache.

MEDICINAL USES
Lime oil shares many of the characteristics of Lemon oil, and is used in aromatherapy as anti-rheumatic, anti-scorbutic, antiseptic, anti-viral, aperitif, bactericidal, febrifuge, restorative, and tonic.

CULINARY USES
Key Lime Pie

Linaloe or Copal Limon

LATIN NAME   Bursera glabrifolia
FAMILY   Burseraceae

           PLANET   Moon

MEDICINAL USES
Folklore has it that the tree must be lacerated on the night of the Full Moon to produce the oil, which can be distilled from the wood only when the tree is 20-30 years old. It is used in aromatherapy for acne, cuts, wounds, nervous tension, and stress.

Lime blossom

Lime or Linden

LATIN NAME	Tilia x vulgaris Hayne	POLARITY	Masculine
FAMILY	Tiliaceae	ELEMENT	Water
FOLK NAMES	Lini, Teili, Tillet, White Wood	PLANET	Jupiter
		RUNE	Ior

ETYMOLOGY   Lime from OE line, from Germanic linden, a serpent

VARIETIES

The Common Lime (Tilia x vulgaris) is a natural hybrid between the Small-leaved Lime (T. cordata) and the Large-leaved Lime (T. platyphyllos). Another variety is the Caucasian Lime (T. x euchlora Koch), often found in towns and on roadsides, due to its high resistance to pollution.

MAGICAL USES

A mark-tree; the village tree representing the cosmic axis, placed at geomantically important points such as crossroads. In Lithuania, women used to sacrifice to lime trees for good crops (men sacrificed to oak trees). In Germany, it was traditionally the tree under which justice was dispensed, and was often used as a gallows, or planted in the middle of turf mazes, and pollarded to resemble Yggdrasil, the world tree. The famous street in Berlin, Unter den Linden, was originally the sacred highway of the Kaisers. Good luck charms were carved from lime wood.

MEDICINAL USES

Lime-flower tea (tilleul) was once used to treat epilepsy. It is also good for indigestion and as a general tonic. Culpeper said it was good for apoplexy, vertigo, and palpitations of the heart. Lime blossom is used in beauty preparations to soothe the skin; and mixed with lavender, makes a good filling for a herbal pillow to help insomniacs sleep. Aromatherapy oil derived from lime flowers is used for cramps, indigestion, liverpains, headaches, insomnia, migraine, nervous tension, and stress.

MYTHOLOGY

In Greek myth, Cronos changed himself into a stallion and sired the centaur Chiron on the sea-nymph Philyra, who was so ashamed of her progeny that she implored the gods to turn her into a tree. She was turned into a lime tree (Philyra in Greek).

SYMBOLISM
Lime symbolises feminine grace, beauty, and happiness. It is a Greek emblem of Baucis, with Philemon as the oak.

CRAFT USES
Lime wood is excellent for intricate carving (much of the work of Grinling Gibbons, the 17th century woodcarver, was executed in lime). Lime is also used to make hat blocks, shoe-lasts, artificial limbs, piano keys, and beehive frames. The bast, or inner bark, is used to make matting, ropes, shoe tops, and clothes.

CULINARY USES
Sugar can be made from lime sap; honey from lime pollen is very popular; tea can be made from the flowers, and they are used to flavour sweets and liqueurs.

Magnolia

LATIN NAME	Magnolia grandifolia	POLARITY	Feminine
FAMILY	Magnoliaceae	ELEMENT	Earth
FOLK NAMES	Blue Magnolia, Cucumber Tree, Swamp Sassafras	PLANET	Venus

VARIETIES
There are about 80 species in the Magnolia family of evergreen shrubs and trees.

MAGICAL USES
Magnolia blossoms placed near or beneath the bed are said to maintain a faithful relationship.

Mandarin or Tangerine

LATIN NAME	Citrus reticulata	POLARITY	Masculine
FAMILY	Rutaceae	ELEMENT	Fire
		PLANET	Sun

MEDICINAL USES
Tangerine oil is used in aromatherapy as an antiseptic, antispasmodic, digestive, mild

127

diuretic and laxative, sedative, tonic, and a stimulant of the digestive and lymphatic systems. It could be used as a substitute for orange in incenses.

Common or Field Maple

LATIN NAME	Acer campestre	POLARITY	Masculine
FAMILY	Aceraceae	ELEMENT	Air
FOLK NAME	Maplin	PLANET	Jupiter
		DEITY	Heimdall
ETYMOLOGY	from Celtic mapwl	RUNE	Man/Mannaz

VARIETIES
Norway Maple (A. platanoides)

MAGICAL USES
The wassailing bowls used at Midwinter were made from maplin (maple wood). To gain a long life, children were passed through the branches of a maple tree.

MEDICINAL USES
According to Culpeper, a decoction of the leaves or bark eases liver pain.

SYMBOLISM
The maple leaf is the emblem of Canada. In Chinese and Japanese symbolism, the maple denotes autumn and lovers.

RHYMES & SONGS

Worcestershire St. Thomas's Day Song

Wassail, wassail, all over the town,
Our toast is white, our ale is brown,
Our bowl is made of a maplin tree;
We be good fellows all - I drink to Thee!

Early 17th c. wassail bowl recipe: "Boil three pints of ale; beat six eggs, the whites and yolks together; set both to the fire in a pewter pot; add roasted apples, honey, beaten nutmegs, clover, and ginger; and being well brewed, drink it hot."
(N.B. Eggs may be omitted and cider substituted for beer.)

CRAFT USES
The timber is ideal for turnery and carving, and takes a high polish.

CULINARY USES
Maple sap can be made into maple syrup and wine.

Mastic

LATIN NAME   Pistacia lentiscus
FAMILY   Anacardiaceae

Gum mastic is used in incense; it is used medicinally in the East for diarrhoea in children, and chewed to sweeten the breath. In aromatherapy the oil is used as antimicrobial, antiseptic, antispasmodic, expectorant, diuretic, and stimulant. The gum is used in the East for sweets and cordials.

Mimosa

POLARITY	Feminine		
LATIN NAME	Acacia dealbata	ELEMENT	Water
FAMILY	Mimosaceae	PLANET	Saturn
FOLK NAME	Black Sydney Wattle		

MAGICAL USES
Purification, love, healing, prophetic dreams(placed under the pillow). Bathing in mimosa is said to destroy hexes and curses and give protection.

MEDICINAL USES
In aromatherapy it is used for oil for sensitive skin, anxiety, nervous tension, over-sensitivity, and stress.

CRAFT USES
The bark contains up to 42% tannins, and is used in the tanning industry.

Mistletoe

LATIN NAME	Viscum album	POLARITY	Masculine
FAMILY	Loranthaceae	ELEMENT	Air
FOLK NAMES	Uchelwydd (Welsh), All Heal, Birdlime, Devil's Fuge, Holy Wood, Thunderbesom, Witches' Broom, Wood of the Cross.	PLANET DEITY	Sun Balder
ETYMOLOGY	OE misteltan, meaning basil twig	RUNE	Sigel /Sowelu

BOTANICAL INFORMATION

Mistletoe is not actually a biological tree, but since it is associated with trees and was regarded as one for magical purposes, I have included it. It is a parasite, growing mainly on apple trees, poplars, willows, and hawthorns, and only rarely on oak trees.

MAGICAL USES

The white berries represented the semen of the sky-god to the Druids, who gave it to the people to hang over their house door as a charm. The Christmas tradition of kissing under the mistletoe is a continuation of this. Mistletoe is burned as an incense to banish evil. It is used as a protective charm against lightning, and fastened to children's cradles to prevent them being taken by the faeries and replaced with a changeling. A ring carved of mistletoe was worn to ward off sickness. Mistletoe is carried for good luck in hunting, and worn by would-be parents to aid in conception. It is said to give restful sleep and beautiful dreams.

MEDICINAL USES

According to Culpeper, mistletoe is useful for epilepsy, fits, convulsions, sores, and ulcers.

FOLKLORE

A sprig of mistletoe was carried to the high altar of York Minster every Christmas until the Reformation, and public liberty, pardon, and freedom was pronounced.

MYTHOLOGY

The King of the Wood at Nemi had to be killed with a dart of mistletoe. Balder, the Norse sun god, was killed by a dart of mistletoe. He had hidden his soul in the mistletoe, because being neither of the earth nor of the sky, the mistletoe was a safe hiding place. Similarly, the life of the oak is said to be in the mistletoe because it is green when the oak is not. Also it is believed that the mistletoe grows where the oak has been struck by lightning, so that it is a gift from the sky-god. As such, it was not permitted to touch the earth; the Druids caught it in a white cloth when they cut it. They gathered it on the sixth day after the New Moon, sacrificing two white bulls and cutting it with a golden sickle. The priest who cut the mistletoe would be dressed in a white robe (hence the popular image of white-robed Druids). The Druids believed that the plant was an universal healer, and would make barren animals bring forth, and was a remedy against all poison. The mistletoe growing on oaks was deemed the most efficacious. Pliny (probably writing of Italian folk-custom) recorded the following taboos about mistletoe: it should not be gathered with iron, nor permitted to touch the earth. If thus obtained, and gathered on the first day of the moon, it was deemed a cure for epilepsy, a means of assisting women to conceive, a means of healing ulcers if the sufferer chewed one piece and laid another on the sore, and a means of extinguishing a fire. The Aino in Japan hold similar beliefs about mistletoe growing on willow trees; in addition, they believe that a sprinkling of mistletoe leaves will make their gardens bear plentifully. In Sweden, mistletoe gathered on Midsummer's Eve is attached to the ceiling of house, stable, and byre to protect them from trolls. In Wales, it is considered to be lucky, and there is a saying, "No mistletoe, no luck".

SYMBOLISM

Life-essence, divine substance, panacea (all-heal), immortality. As being neither tree nor shrub it symbolises things which are neither one thing nor another, hence freedom from limitation, but also absence of protection, entering into the world of chaos. It symbolises the sacred feminine principle, where the oak is the masculine principle; it is the anima of the oak-god. It is called the Golden Bough because it was believed to be an emanation of the sun's fire, hence it was held to extinguish fire.

RHYMES & SONGS

In Scotland the fortunes of the Hay family were said to have been bound up with mistletoe on Errol's Oak. It is said that when the oak was cut down, the estate was sold out of the family:

"While the mistletoe bats on Errol's aik,
And that aik stands fast,

The Hays shall flourish, and their good grey hawk
Shall nocht flinch before the blast.

But when the root of the aik decays,
And the mistletoe dwines on its withered breast,
The grass shall grow on Errol's hearthstane,
And the corbie roup in the falcon's nest."

(attributed to Thomas the Rhymer)

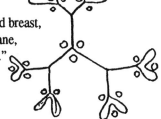

Black Mulberry

LATIN NAME	Morus nigra	POLARITY	Feminine
FAMILY	Moraceae	ELEMENT	Air
FOLK NAMES	Sycamine, sikmah	PLANET	Mercury
ETYMOLOGY	from OE morberie, ultimately from Latin morus		

VARIETIES

There is also the White Mulberry
(M. alba), and 10 other species,
including the Paper Mulberry
(Broussonetia papyrifera).

MAGICAL USES

The mulberry is a tree of life and is
deemed to be a protection against the powers of darkness.

MEDICINAL USES

According to Culpeper, the unripe berries are useful to stay bleeding, whilst the juice
from the ripe berries is good for a sore throat, and a decoction of the bark and leaves
is good for toothache.

MYTHOLOGY

In Greek myth, mulberry represents misfortune in love, as the mingled blood of
Pyramus and Thisbe. The tree climbed by the man in Luke 17:6 who wanted to see
Jesus but was too short to see over the heads of the crowd was not in fact a sycamore,
but a sycamine (from Hebrew sikmah) or mulberry tree. In the month of Khoiak in

Egypt the rites of Osiris culminated in the burial of an effigy of Osiris in a mulberry-wood coffin and the removal of the previous year's effigy to the boughs of a sycamore fig tree.

SYMBOLISM

The three colours of the three stages of the ripening of the berries are white, red, and black, representing the Triple Goddess (Maiden, Mother, and Crone), the three stages of initiation, and the three stages of life (white, the innocence of the child; red, the active adult; and black, old age and death). The mulberry also represents industry and filial piety.

RHYMES & SONGS

"Here we go round the mulberry-tree..."
(Nursery rhyme)

"Mulberry-tree. Love's lack hath dyed my berries red:
For Love's attire my leaves are shed."

(from "Tapestry Trees", by William Morris)

CRAFT USES

The Paper Mulberry (Broussonetia papyrifera) is used in paper-making and in the manufacture of tapa cloth in Polynesia. The timber of the Black and the White Mulberry is used for ornamental work, inlays, and turnery, but not much timber can be obtained from any one tree. Silk-worms feed on the leaves of the mulberry tree.

CULINARY USES

The fruits resemble raspberries and can be used to make preserves.

Myrrh

LATIN NAME	Commiphora myrrha	POLARITY	Feminine
FAMILY	Burseraceae	ELEMENT	Water
		PLANET	Moon
		DEITIES	Isis, Ra, Adonis

MAGICAL USES

Myrrh was burned at noon in Egypt in honour of Ra, and also in the temples of Isis. It is used as a purificatory incense, often in combination with frankincense. It is a healing and consecratory incense, and aids meditation.

MEDICINAL USES

Myrrh was used by the Egyptians for embalming, perfumes, and cosmetics. The Chinese used it for arthritis, menstrual problems, sores, and haemorrhoids. In the West it was used for coughs, asthma, colds, ulcers, sores, and weak gums and teeth. It is used in aromatherapy for all these purposes (except embalming, obviously).

FOLKLORE

Myrrh was one of the gifts of the Three Kings or Magi (see FRANKINCENSE), symbolising Christ as Divine Physician. It is interesting that both frankincense and myrrh were burned in honour of Ra (Egyptian sun god), who, in the reign of Amenhotep IV of Egypt (who changed his name to Akhenaton) was worshipped as the one and only deity; this development is said to be the origin of the monotheism of the Hebrews, who became a persecuted minority in Egypt after the restoration of polytheism; the two substances plus gold, the metal of the sun, would have been entirely appropriate gifts for the son of a sun god.

Seville Orange or Neroli

LATIN NAME	Citrus aurantium	POLARITY	Masculine
FAMILY	Rutaceae	ELEMENT	Fire
FOLK NAME	Bitter orange	PLANET	Sun

VARIETIES

Neroli is a member of the genus Citrus, which includes orange, lemon, and lime.

MEDICINAL USES

Essential oil of Neroli is used for relieving depression in a massage oil or fragrancer. It is also good for insomnia, hysteria, anxiety, and states of shock. It acts as a tonic on the skin.

CULINARY USES

Seville oranges are used to make marmalade.

Niaouli

LATIN NAME   Melaleuca viridiflora
FAMILY   Myrtaceae   PLANET   Jupiter

MEDICINAL USES
Closely related to cajeput and ti tree (q.v.), niaouli is used in aromatherapy for cystitis, urinary infections, aches and pains, rheumatism, colds, coughs, and catarrh.

Nutmeg

LATIN NAME   Myristica fragrans   POLARITY   Masculine
FAMILY   Myristicaceae   ELEMENT   Fire
                            PLANET   Jupiter

MAGICAL USES
The red outer husk of the nutmeg is mace (polarity, masculine; element, air; planet, Mercury) which is used in incense to increase psychic powers and carried to increase intellect. Nutmeg itself is carried as a good luck charm and used in a spell for fidelity; it is also carried to ward off neuralgia, cold sores, boils, and styes. It is hung from a string around a baby's neck to aid teething.

MEDICINAL USES
The aromatherapy oil is used for arthritis, muscle pain, flatulence, indigestion, impotence, neuralgia, fatigue, and bacterial infections.

CULINARY USES
Both nutmeg and mace are used as a spice. Mace is used in men's perfumes.

Common or Pedunculate Oak

LATIN NAME	Quercus robur	POLARITY	Masculine
FAMILY	Fagaceae	ELEMENT	Air/Earth
FOLK NAME	Jove's nuts	PLANET	Jupiter
		DEITIES	Tiw, Balder, Jupiter, Juno, Silvanus, Cybele, Thor, Perkunas
ETYMOLOGY	from OE ac, from the Germanic	RUNES	Tyr/Teiwaz, Rad/Raido, Ger/Jera, Eh/Ehwaz.
		OGHAM	Duir

VARIETIES

Sessile or Durmast Oak (Q. petraea); Turkey Oak (Q. cerris); Cork Oak (Q. suber); American Red Oak (Q. rubra); Pin Oak (Q. palustris); Scarlet Oak (Q. coccinea); and Holm or Evergreen Oak (Q. ilex). There is also a hybrid between the Common Oak and the Holm Oak called Turner's Oak (Q. x turnerii).

Oak

MAGICAL USES

The acorn is carved on the end of wands. Oak trees were planted in sacred groves by the Druids. The timber was used in building to ward off lightning, especially if the tree whence it came had already been struck by lightning (because lightning is said never to strike in the same place twice). Similarly, acorns were carved on banisters and blind-pull bobbins to ward off lightning. Lithuanian men sacrificed to oak trees for good crops, and the oak was considered oracular in pagan Lithuania. The oracle of Zeus listened to the whispering of the wind through the leaves of the sacred oak-grove at Dodona; in Arcadia an oak-branch from the sacred grove of Zeus was dipped into a sacred spring to bring rain. Lycaean Zeus was similarly used; in periods of drought, his priest would touch the surface of the fountain ruled by the nymph Hago with an oak branch; at once a mist would arise, become a cloud, and bring rain. Acorns were carried to ward off illness and ensure long life. Oak was also used to get rid of gout, by placing the sufferer's fingernail-parings and leg-hairs into a hole bored in the trunk, which was then stopped up again and smeared with cow-dung. Two oak

136

twigs bound with red thread to form an equal-armed cross are hung in the house to ward off evil. Catching a falling oak-leaf is said to ensure that you will get no colds all winter. An oak fire is said to draw off illness from a sick person. An acorn planted at the dark of the moon is said to ensure a supply of money in the near future; carrying an acorn is said to increase potency. Oak is generally regarded as the king of the woods and should not be burnt in any sacred fire (unless you are Lithuanian - see MYTHOLOGY).

MEDICINAL USES

Culpeper used the powdered bark and acorn cups to stay bleeding and vomiting. Powdered acorn in wine was used as a diuretic.

Unleached acorns will purge the intestinal tract of excess flora and fauna, including dysentery. Oak is astringent, tonic, and antiseptic; it is used for chronic diarrhoea and dysentery, and as a gargle for chronic sore throat. It can also be applied locally to piles and bleeding gums.

FOLKLORE

The Yule Log can be made of oak. St. Augustine's first sermon was preached under an oak. King Ethelbert of England always received Christian missionaries under an oak to be safe from their malignant magical powers. It is said to be especially fortuitous to be married under an oak. Mistletoe growing on the oak is said to shield it from lightning (it is also said to grow where the tree has been struck by lightning, but as lightning is said never to strike twice in the same place, this would be logical).

SAYINGS

"Mighty oaks from little acorns grow."

"Little strokes fell great oaks." (Benjamin Franklin, Poor Richard's Almanac, 1750)

WEATHER LORE

Oaks attract lightning. If the oak blooms before the ash, it will be a good year; if ash blooms before oak there will be a cold summer and a poor harvest.

MYTHOLOGY

The Oak King (King of the Waxing Year) kills the Holly King (King of the Waning Year) at Yule, and is himself killed at Midsummer by the Holly King. Midsummer Day is St. John's Day in the Christian calendar - St. John the Baptist was equated

137

with the Oak King, and Christ (whose festival, Christmas, was equated with Yule) with the Holly King. In classical mythology, Jupiter was the Oak King, Saturn the Holly King.

The Californian Indians regarded the oak as the World Tree or Cosmic Axis. In the Old World, gods associated with the oak were Yahweh (Jehovah), Zeus, Jupiter, Dagda, Thor, Thunor, Donar, Allah, Taranis, and Perkunas. Zeus wore a crown of oak leaves; Hercules' club was made of oak. It was sacred to Jupiter and Juno; the marriage of the oak-god Jupiter to the oak-goddess Juno was celebrated each year in an oak-grove; the worshippers wore crowns of oak-leaves. In Boeotia they celebrated the sacred marriage of Zeus and Hera (oak-god and oak-goddess) with much pomp and ceremony. The oak is also an emblem of Cybele and of Silvanus. The dryads were oak nymphs. In Scandinavian and Teutonic myth, it was Thor's tree of life, and was also sacred to Donar. Oak groves were places of worship in Germanic ritual. Balder was the Germanic deity of the oak, who could not be killed by anything but a dart of mistletoe. Since the life of the tree is believed to reside in the mistletoe, it must be broken off before the tree can be cut down. The oak was held to represent the sky-god because it is so frequently struck by lightning: a visible entry into the tree by the sky-god himself - hence the respect with which blasted oaks were held in myth and folklore. The oak was also sacred to Pyerun (the pagan prototype of Ilya Muromyets, the bogatyr hero of Russian folk-tales) and the Lithuanian god Perkunas, in whose honour perpetual oak-wood fires were maintained; if they went out they were relit by friction of the sacred wood. Acorns are traditionally fed to pigs, lunar animals sacred to Demeter, Cerridwen, and Freyja.

SYMBOLISM

The acorn is symbolic of the cosmic egg, and of immortality. The oak tree symbolises strength, protection, durability, courage, truth, man, and the human body; also thunder gods, thunder, the sky, and fertility. To some Native Americans, the oak is sacred to the Earth Mother; to the Celts, it was sacred to the Dagda. To the Chinese, it symbolises masculine strength, but also the weakness of the strength which resists and breaks in the storm, in contrast to the strength-in-weakness of the willow, which bends before the storm and survives. In Christian symbolism it denotes Christ as strength in adversity, steadfastness in faith and virtue; and it was said to have been the tree from which the Cross was fashioned. To the Druids it was the sacred tree, the masculine principle, with the mistletoe (q.v.) as feminine. The Graeco-Roman custom was to award crowns of oak leaves for saving life and for victory in the Pythian Games. In Greece it is a symbol of Philemon as conjugal devotion and happiness. To the Hebrews, it represented the Tree of the Covenant, the Divine Presence. The Ogham Duir (oak) represents the door of the year; oakwood is often used to make doors.

Oak

139

RHYMES & SONGS

"Oak before ash, we're in for a splash
Ash before oak, we're in for a soak."

"Oak logs will warm you well
That are old and dry."
(Dartmoor folk song)

"An oak is three hundred years growing,
Three hundred years blowing,
And three hundred years decaying." (Country saying)

"Oak. I am the Roof-tree and the Keel:
I bridge the seas for woe and weal."
(from "Tapestry Trees" by William Morris)

" -...   at intervals,
The mythic oaks and elm-trees stand,
Self-poised upon their prodigy of shade"
(from "The Sweetness of England" by Elizabeth Barrett Browning)

Song of the Cauld Lad of Hilton   (Anon.)

"Wae's me, wae's me,
The acorn is not yet
Fallen from a tree
That's to grow the wood
That's to make the cradle
That's to rock the bairn
That's to grow to a man
That's to slay me."

CRAFT USES
Oak galls can be used to make ink. The timber is used for doors, roof-beams, boats, furniture, gates, fence posts, coffins, and veneers. The bark can be used for tanning. Different parts of the tree yield black, brown, red, and yellow dyes.

CULINARY USES
The sweeter acorns can be roasted, while the more bitter need to be leached in cold

running water for a couple of days to get rid of the tannin. The kernel may be eaten raw, roasted, or ground into flour. Very bitter acorns can be used to catch fish: if the stream is dammed and the acorns thrown in, the tannin in them will stupefy the fish, which will rise to the surface; when the dam is removed any fish not taken will recover and swim on.

The food value of an acorn is: 5.2% protein; 43% fat; 45% carbohydrates; and 6.3% water.

Olive

LATIN NAME	Olea europaea	POLARITY	Masculine
FAMILY	Oleaceae	ELEMENT	Fire
		PLANET	Moon
		DEITIES	Athena, Apollo, Irene, Minerva, Ra

VARIETIES
Related to Ash (q.v.) and Privet.

MAGICAL USES
Olive oil was burnt in temple lamps in ancient times; it was also used as an anointing oil to aid in healing. Olive leaves are scattered to bring peace and tranquillity. The fruit is said to be an aphrodisiac; Athenian brides wore crowns of olive leaves to ensure fertility. Olive branches are hung over doors to ward off evil and over chimneys to ward off lightning. Olive leaves are worn for luck.

MYTHOLOGY .
In Greek myth, the olive tree owed its fruit to Athene. As part of the Panathenea festival, old men carried olive branches to the Acropolis. The olive tree which grew at the Acropolis held the life and fate of the people. The olive was also sacred to Apollo. A crown of olives worn by the victor at the Heraea identified the victorious virgin with Hera and the Moon. The crown of wild olives for the victor at the Olympic Games represented Zeus; the two together symbolised the sacred marriage of Zeus and Hera, Sun and Moon.

SYMBOLISM
Immortality, fruitfulness, fertility, peace, plenty. A dove carrying an olive branch is symbolic of peace and the golden age. The olive tree is an emblem of the Moon. The

olive leaf denotes the renewal of life. In Chinese symbolism the olive denotes quietness, persistence, grace, and delicacy. In Christianity, it represents the fruit of the Church, the faith of the just, and peace; the dove with the olive twig denotes the souls of the faithful departed in peace. The Archangel Gabriel was sometimes depicted carrying an olive-branch in pictures of the Annunciation. In Graeco-Roman symbolism, it denoted achievement and peace; to the Hebrews, it was strength, beauty, and safe travel.

RHYMES & SONGS

"Olive. The King I bless; the lamps I trim;
In my warm wave do fishes swim."

(from "Tapestry Trees" by William Morris)

CULINARY USES
The olive and its oil is used extensively in Mediterranean cookery. Vegetables fried in olive oil have a cleaner, more pleasant taste; olive oil is also used to make bread. The fruits are often used in pizza toppings or added to vegetables to impart an interesting flavour.

Opoponax, Opopanax

LATIN NAME	Commiphora erythraea	POLARITY	Feminine
FAMILY	Burseraceae	ELEMENT	Water
FOLK NAME	Sponge tree	PLANET	Moon
ETYMOLOGY	Greek opos, juice, + panax, from panacea		

MAGICAL USES
Opoponax is used as an ingredient in incense.

MEDICINAL USES
Opoponax is used similarly to myrrh (q.v.) in aromatherapy. In folk medicine, it is used as an antispasmodic, expectorant, emmenagogue, and antiseptic for asthma, hysteria, and visceral conditions.

Orange

LATIN NAME	Citrus sinensis	POLARITY	Masculine
FAMILY	Rutaceae	ELEMENT	Fire
FOLK NAME	Love fruit	PLANET	Sun
		DEITY	Diana
ETYMOLOGY	ME from Old French orenge from Arabic naranj from Persian narang		

VARIETIES

The orange is a member of the family Rutaceae, which includes lemon, lime, and bitter orange (Neroli).

MAGICAL USES

Oranges are used in love charms and sachets; also in divination - eat an orange, thinking of the question you want answered, and then count the seeds. An even number means no, an odd number yes. Drinking an infusion of orange peel is said to prevent drunkenness.

MEDICINAL USES

The fruit is rich in Vitamin C.

FOLKLORE

Orange blossom is traditionally carried by brides.

MYTHOLOGY

It is thought that the Golden Apples of the Hesperides may have been oranges.

SYMBOLISM

Orange blossom is a symbol of fertility and fruitfulness; it was worn by Saracen brides to signify fecundity. To the Chinese it represents immortality and good fortune. In Christianity it is purity, chastity, and virginity, and is used as a bridal wreath to signify this. The fruit, if depicted in Paradise, symbolises the Fall; it is sometimes portrayed in the hand of the Christ Child instead of the apple. To the Greeks, it was an emblem of Diana. To the Japanese, the blossom denotes pure love.

RHYMES & SONGS

"Oranges and lemons,
Say the bells of St. Clement's."
(Nursery rhyme)

"Orange-tree. Amidst the greenness of my night
My odorous lamps hang round and bright."
(from "Tapestry Trees" by William Morris)

Orange
☉

CULINARY USES
Orange juice; orange sorbet, etc. Orange oil is the main ingredient of the liqueur Blue Curacao.

Osier

LATIN NAME	Salix viminalis	POLARITY Feminine
FAMILY	Salicaceae	ELEMENT Water
FOLK NAMES	Various, according to the	PLANET Moon
	quality of the rods (see	DEITIES Njord,Nerthus
	CRAFT USES)	RUNE Lagu /Laguz
ETYMOLOGY	ME from Old French from	
	medieval Latin auseria,	OGHAM Saille
	an osier bed	

VARIETIES
Almond-leaved Willow (S. triandra); Purple Osier (S. purpurea); Creeping Willow (S. repens)

SYMBOLISM
Osier symbolises purification and rebirth.

CRAFT USES
The coppiced shoots are used in the making of baskets, lobster pots, fish traps, bird cages, hurdles, and, after 2-3 years' growth, coopers' hoops. Osier rods are called by different names according to quality, e.g. black mauls, green sucklings, black hollander, glibskins.

Papaya

LATIN NAME	Carica papaya	POLARITY	Feminine
FAMILY	Caricaceae	ELEMENT	Water
FOLK NAME	Papaw, pawpaw	PLANET	Moon
ETYMOLOGY	from a Caribbean word		

MAGICAL USES

A simple magical rite was to tie a piece of rag round a papaya tree whilst visualising a need. Twigs of papaya wood hung over the doorsill are said to keep evil from entering the house. The fruit shared with a loved one is said to intensify the feelings of love.

CULINARY USES

The fruits are eaten fresh, boiled, or in preserves and pickles; they are a commercial source of the enzyme papain.

Peach

LATIN NAME	Prunus persica	POLARITY	Feminine
FAMILY	Rosaceae	ELEMENT	Water
ETYMOLOGY	ultimately from Latin	PLANET	Venus
	persica, meaning Persian	DEITY	Si Wang Mu

VARIETIES

Peach is a member of the Rosaceae family, related to almond, pear, apple, blackthorn, etc. Its closest relative is the nectarine (P. persica var. nectarina).

MAGICAL USES

The fruit is said to induce love and give the eater wisdom when eaten. In China, peach branches were used to drive off evil spirits and to root out illness. Chinese children were given peach pit necklaces to drive demons away. Carrying peach wood is said to increase one's life-span. The Japanese use the peach to increase fertility, and the branches are used as divining rods. The Taoists carve peach stones and use them as amulets and talismans.

MEDICINAL USES

Culpeper used a conserve made from the leaves or flowers of the peach tree to purge choler and jaundice. The fruit, according to him, provokes lust; bruised leaves laid on the abdomen killed worms, whilst boiled in ale and drunk, could cure constipation. He used powdered leaves to stay the bleeding of fresh wounds, and close them up; syrup made from the flowers to provoke vomiting; the sap with a decoction of coltsfoot for a sore throat; oil from the kernels applied to the temples for migraine; and the kernels bruised and boiled in vinegar until thick for baldness.

SYMBOLISM

To the Buddhists, the peach (with the citron and the pomegranate) is one of the Three Blessed Fruits. To the Chinese, it is immortality, the Tree of Life, faery fruit, Spring, youth, marriage, riches, long life, and good wishes. In Christianity it is the fruit of salvation; a peach with a leaf attached denotes virtue of heart and tongue, or the virtue of silence. In Egyptian myth it was sacred to Hathor and Harpocrates. To the Japanese it is the Tree of Immortality; the blossom denotes Spring, feminine charm, and marriage. To the Taoists it is the Tree of Life in the Kun-lun Paradise; it bestows immortality and is the food of the Taoist genii or immortals. The peach with the phoenix is an emblem of Si Wang Mu, goddess of the Tree of Immortality and Queen of Heaven.

CULINARY USES

Peach wine and liqueurs.

Pear

LATIN NAME	Pyrus communis		POLARITY	Feminine
FAMILY	Rosaceae		ELEMENT	Water
ETYMOLOGY	OE pere, peru, from Latin pirus		PLANET	Venus

VARIETIES

The genus Pyrus has 20 species of deciduous, hardy, flowering and fruitbearing trees and shrubs.

MAGICAL USES

In Switzerland, when a girl was born, it used to be the custom to plant a pear tree for her (apple trees were planted for boys). In Circassia the pear tree was worshipped as

146

the protector of cattle. In Slavonic countries pear-wood was used to kindle need-fires.

MEDICINAL USES

It is good for applying to 'green wounds' according to Culpeper, and to cool and stay the blood. Boiled with honey, it settles the stomach.

SYMBOLISM

Pear symbolises hope and good health; to the Chinese, it represents longevity, justice, good government, and good judgement. In Christianity it symbolises the love of Christ for humanity.

RHYMES & SONGS

"Pear-tree. High o'er the mead-flowers' hidden feet
I bear aloft my burden sweet.
(from "Tapestry Trees" by William Morris)

CULINARY USES

The fruit can be used to make pear wine.

Pecan

LATIN NAME	Carya illinoensis	POLARITY	Masculine
FAMILY	Juglandaceae	ELEMENT	Air
ETYMOLOGY	from Algonquin paccan	PLANET	Mercury

MAGICAL USES

Pecans are used in money or prosperity spells. They are also used in a spell to make sure that one keeps one's job, in which the pecans are shelled and eaten, whilst visualising oneself working and enjoying the job; then the shells are put in a bag and put somewhere whence they will not be removed.

CULINARY USES

Pecan Pie

147

Pepper tree

LATIN NAME	Schinus molle		POLARITY	Masculine
FAMILY	Anacardiaceae		ELEMENT	Mars
			PLANET	Fire

MAGICAL USES
The branches are used by Mexican curanderos (medicine men) in healing rituals. They brush the person with the branch to absorb the disease, then bury the branch to destroy it. The red berries are carried for protection, and the leaves are added to purificatory baths.

MEDICINAL USES
The oil of the pepper tree is used in aromatherapy as antiseptic, anti-viral, bactericidal, carminative,stimulant, and stomachic.

CULINARY USES
In Greece and the Mediterranean countries, an intoxicating beverage is made from the fruits of the tree. The fruit is also used as a substitute for pepper in these countries.

Persimmon

LATIN NAME	Diospyros spp.		POLARITY	Feminine
FAMILY	Ebenaceae		ELEMENT	Water
ETYMOLOGY	from an Algonquin word		PLANET	Venus

VARIETIES
American Persimmon (D. virginiana); Japanese Persimmon (D. kaki); Asian Date Plum (D. lotus)

MAGICAL USES
In Alabama it was believed that a girl could change into a boy by eating nine unripe persimmons. The change would occur, it was said, within two weeks. People plagued with chills would tie knots in a string, one for each afflicted area, and tie the string to a persimmon tree. Good luck was said to result from burying green (unripe) persimmons.

CULINARY USES
Persimmons can be eaten fresh, cooked, or candied.

Scots Pine

LATIN NAME	Pinus sylvestris	POLARITY	Masculine
FAMILY	Pinaceae	ELEMENT	Fire/Air
ETYMOLOGY	ultimately from Latin pinus	PLANET	Sun/Mars
		DEITY	Freyr
		RUNE	Kano/Ken
		OGHAM	Ao

VARIETIES
Maritime or Cluster Pine (P. pinaster); Coastal Lodgepole or Beach Pine (P. contorta); Western Hemlock Tree (Tsuga heterophylla); Eastern Hemlock (T. canadensis); Mountain Hemlock (T. mertensiana).

MAGICAL USES
Pine cones (deal apples) are stuck to the end of wands as a symbol of fertility. The resin makes a good incense. The cones are carried to increase fertility and for a vigorous old age. A pine cone plucked on Midsummer's Eve, and one kernel from it eaten every day, is said to make one impervious to gunshot wounds. Pine needles are burned during the winter months to purify the house of negativity. Scattered on the floor, they are said to drive away evil; they are also used in cleansing baths. Pine branches are placed over invalids' beds to help them recover, and over a well person's bed to keep illness away. In Japan a pine branch is hung over the door of the house to ensure continual joy within (because the pine is an evergreen). The sawdust can also be used as an incense base. Norfolk Island Pine (Auricaria excelsa) is considered to offer protection against hunger and evil spirits when grown in or near the home.

MEDICINAL USES
A medicinal oil is extracted from the needles which is a good antiseptic and analgesic. Pine is used in the Bach flower remedies for those who blame themselves for everything and are never content with their efforts or the results. The oil is used in aromatherapy as antiseptic, anti-viral, bactericidal, deodorant, and diuretic; it is useful in cystitis, urinary tract infections, colds, coughs, and respiratory tract infections, arthritis, gout, and poor circulation.

FOLKLORE

Pine was thought to preserve the body from corruption, so it was used to make coffins.

MYTHOLOGY

The pine cone is an emblem of Zeus and Artemis, Jupiter and Venus; it was also associated with Mithras. Pan seduced the nymph Pitys, who preferred him to Boreas, the North Wind. Boreas flung her against a rock in a jealous fury, crushing her limbs. In pity Gaea transformed her into a pine tree. In the battle between the Centaurs and the Lapiths, the Centaurs were armed with pine trunks and slabs of stone. Hercules was cremated on a funeral pyre of pine wood. The Corinthians made two images of Dionysos from pine; also, Dionysos' thyrsis is tipped with a pine-cone.

There are two accounts of the death of Attis, consort of the goddess Cybele: one is that he was killed by a boar, like Adonis; the other is that he castrated himself beneath a pine tree, and bled to death. The latter would explain why the priests of Attis and Cybele castrated themselves on entering the service of the goddess. After his death Attis is said to have been transformed into a pine tree. There is a statue of him in the Lateran Museum at Rome where he is wearing a wreath of pine-cones, pomegranates, and other fruits. On 22nd March a pine tree was cut down in the woods and brought into the sanctuary of Cybele, where the rites culminated in an orgy of blood-letting by the worshippers. The pine was decorated with bands of wool and violets; an effigy of Attis was bound to it, which was kept for a year and then burned; clearly it embodied the vegetation spirit, which must be renewed every year. In some places in Egypt, an effigy of Osiris was kept in a hollowed-out pine tree, kept for a year and then burnt. (See the section on the Maypole in Chapter One.)

SYMBOLISM

Pine symbolises uprightness, straightness, vitality, strength of character, silence and solitude. It is phallic. As an evergreen it represents immortality. To the Chinese it is an emblem of K'ung Fu-tse (Confucius), and symbolises longevity, courage, faithfulness, and constancy in adversity. With the plum and bamboo, it is one of the Three Friends of Winter. In Indo-European symbolism the pine cone represents fire, the masculine creative force, fecundity and good luck.

CRAFT USES

The tree yields pitch tar, resin, and turpentine. The timber is used in construction for joists, rafters, flooring, window frames, etc. It is also used for pit props, telegraph poles, gate posts, crates, coffins, sleepers, and paper pulp. The North American Indians used the stems of the Coastal Lodgepole or Beach Pine (P. contorta) for their tepee supports; also they used the roots of the Western Hemlock Tree (Tsuga heterophylla) to make fish-hooks.

CULINARY USES
The kernels of the cones can be eaten, and are a good source of protein. The North American Indians used the inner bark of the Western Hemlock Tree to make a type of bread.

Pistachio

LATIN NAME	Pistacia vera	POLARITY	Masculine
FAMILY	Anacardiaceae	ELEMENT	Air
ETYMOLOGY	From Persian pistah	PLANET	Mercury

MAGICAL USES
The Arabs believe eating pistachios to be an antidote to love spells. The red-dyed nuts are given to zombies to break their trance and give them the repose of death.

CULINARY USES
Used to flavour kulfi (Indian ice-cream), halva (Middle Eastern sweetmeat), ice-cream, sweets, etc.

London Plane

LATIN NAME	Platanus x hispanica	POLARITY	Masculine
FAMILY	Platanaceae	ELEMENT	Air
ETYMOLOGY	ME from Old French from Latinplatanus from Greek platanos from platus, meaning broad	PLANET	Jupiter
		DEITY	Cretan Zeus

VARIETIES
The London Plane is generally considered to be a cross between the Oriental Plane (P. orientalis) and the Western Plane (P. occidentalis).

MYTHOLOGY

Roman orators and statesmen used to return home at midday to offer wine to their plane trees. The great commander Xerxes stopped his army of two million men to admire a plane tree, then had it covered in precious metals and gems. At Magnesia on the river Maeander an image  of Dionysos was found in a plane tree which had been broken by the wind. The plane tree is sacred to Zeus because he, assuming the form of a bull, carried off Europa (daughter of Phoenix or Agenor, King of Phoenicia and Telephassa); Europa was gathering flowers with her friends by the sea when she caught sight of the bull, by which she was enchanted; she hung a wreath of flowers on its horns and playfully climbed on its back, whereupon it charged off across the sea, coming to a stop at Gortyna in Crete, where the plane tree witnessed the divine union (the rape of Europa). Because of this the plane tree was given the privilege of having foliage all year round.

SYMBOLISM

To the Christians, the plane symbolises the all-embracing love of Christ, charity, and morality. To the Greeks it represents learning and scholarship; academic discussions in Athens were held under a plane tree. To the Iranians it represented magnificence and learning. In Minoan Crete it was sacred to Zeus (see MYTHOLOGY).

CRAFT USES

Plane wood is used for joinery, doors, floor blocks, furniture, veneers, decorative carving, turnery, and lacewood (cut to display its silver grain).

Plum

LATIN NAME	Prunus domestica	POLARITY	Feminine
FAMILY	Rosaceae	ELEMENT	Water
ETYMOLOGY	OE plume from medieval	PLANET	Venus
	Latin pruna from Latin	DEITY	Shou-hsing
	prunus		(Chinese god of
			longevity)

VARIETIES
The plum cultivated in Britain is a natural hybrid between the sloe or blackthorn (P. spinosa) and the cherry plum (P. cerasifera). The closest relative of the plum is the damson (P. institia).

MAGICAL USES
Plum branches are placed over doors and windows to protect the home from evil intrusions. The fruit is eaten to inspire or maintain love. The Dakota Indians used wild plum (P. americana) sprouts to make prayer sticks. The sprouts were peeled and painted, and an offering of tobacco placed at the top. They represented prayers for invalids and were stuck in the ground for the gods or set up around the altar.

MEDICINAL USES
According to Culpeper, the fruit loosens the bowels; the leaves boiled in wine are good to get rid of excessive phlegm; the gum and/or the leaves boiled in vinegar kills ringworm and mitigates the effects of eczema.

SYMBOLISM
In Christianity the plum represents independence and fidelity. To the Japanese, the blossom symbolises Spring triumphant over Winter; virtue and courage triumphing over difficulty; marriage and happiness. The tree is also an emblem of the Samurai. To the Chinese, plum symbolises longevity, Winter, beauty, purity, and the recluse. The unripe fruit symbolise pupils. Because the plum flowers in winter, it represents strength, endurance, and triumph. With the bamboo and the pine, it is one of the Three Friends of Winter.

CULINARY USES
Plum wine.

Pomegranate

LATIN NAME	Punica granatum	POLARITY	Masculine
FAMILY	Punicaceae	ELEMENT	Fire
ETYMOLOGY	from French pomme	PLANET	Mercury
	grenade	DEITY	Ceres,
			Kore, Persephone

MAGICAL USES

The seeds are eaten and the skin carried to increase fertility. Some people make a wish before eating a pomegranate. A branch of pomegranate is used to discover concealed wealth or to attract money. Women throw pomegranates on the ground to discover how many children they will have; the number of seeds that fall out denotes the number of children. The branches are hung over doors for protection. The juice of the fruit is used as a magical ink. Witches eat pomegranates at Hallowe'en to symbolise going down into the Underworld.

MYTHOLOGY

In the myth of Persephone's abduction by Hades, he offers her a pomegranate. She eats six seeds, which means she must stay in the Underworld for six months of the year, but, at her mother Demeter's pleading to the Gods of Olympus, spends the other six on Earth.

SYMBOLISM

The pomegranate was a symbol of conjugal love and fruitfulness to the Greeks, and as such an emblem of Hera. Persephone's attributes were the bat, the narcissus, and the pomegranate. In general the pomegranate symbolises immortality, multiplicity in unity, perennial fertility, fecundity, and plenty. To the Buddhists it is (with the citron and the peach) one of the Three Blessed Fruits. To the Chinese it is abundance, fertility, posterity, numerous and virtuous offspring, and a happy future. In Christianity it is eternal life, spiritual fecundity, and the Church (the seeds being the members of the Church). In Graeco-Roman symbolism it is Spring, rejuvenation, immortality, fertility, an emblem of Juno, Ceres, and Persephone as the periodic return of Spring and fertility to the Earth. It is also the plant which grew from the blood of Dionysos. To the Hebrews it was regeneration and fertility; the pomegranates and bells on the priestly vestments symbolised the fecundating power of thunder and lightning. The name 'hand grenade' comes from the French name, pomme grenade, and grenades represented in heraldry often resemble pomegranates.

CULINARY USES
The juice of the pomegranate is the main ingredient of Grenadine liqueur; the seeds can be toasted and eaten.

Poplar

LATIN NAME	Populus spp.	POLARITY	Feminine
FAMILY	Salicaceae	ELEMENT	Earth/Water
FOLK NAME	Abele (White Poplar)	PLANET	Saturn
ETYMOLOGY	ME from Old French	DEITIES	Uller, Hades
	poplier from pople	RUNE	Eolh/Eihwaz
	from Latin populus		

VARIETIES
White Poplar (P. alba); Black Poplar (P. nigra)

MAGICAL USES
Poplar was formerly used for making the shafts of arrows; hence it has divinatory virtues and can be used to make divinatory shields. The buds and leaves are carried to attract money; they are also used in flying ointments, which are used to facilitate astral projection. In Slavonic countries, the poplar, with dogwood and pear, was used to kindle the needfire.

WEATHER LORE
Pliny states that the white poplar always turns its leaves to an opposite quarter of the heavens immediately the summer solstice has passed. When poplars show the underside of their leaves, giving them a lighter appearance than usual, it is a sure sign of wet weather.

MYTHOLOGY
The White Poplar denotes the Elysian Fields, and the Black Poplar denotes Hades. Poplar was sacred to Sabazios (a syncretised deity representing the Dying God in his many forms) and was carried in his rites. Herakles (Hercules) wore a crown of poplar on his descent to Hades.

SYMBOLISM
Emblem of Zeus and Jupiter. To the Chinese, poplar leaves represent yin and yang, the lunar and solar principles, and all dualities

155

RHYMES & SONGS

"Poplar. The war-shaft and the milking-bowl
I make, and keep the haywain whole."
(from "Tapestry Trees" by William Morris)

CRAFT USES

White Poplar is used for flooring, matches, and arrows.

Prickly Ash

LATIN NAME	Xanthoxylum americanum	POLARITY	Masculine
		ELEMENT	Fire
		PLANET	Mars

MAGICAL USES

The fruits of Prickly Ash are used as a perfume to attract love.

Common Privet

LATIN NAME	Ligustrum vulgare	POLARITY	Feminine
FAMILY	Oleaceae	ELEMENT	Earth
ETYMOLOGY	16th c. - origin unknown	PLANET	Moon
		DEITY	Hecate

VARIETIES

Oval-leaved Privet (L. ovalifolium) was introduced from Japan in 1877; Golden Privet is a cultivar of this; and Shining Privet, also known as the Woa Tree (L. lucidum) was introduced to Europe in 1794.

MEDICINAL USES

According to Culpeper, a lotion made from Privet can be used to wash sores and cool inflammation, and a sweet water distilled from the flowers is good for the stomach.

CRAFT USES

The oil from the berries may be used as lamp fuel, and as an ingredient of soap. The twigs are used in tanning, and the shoots can be used to make baskets.

N.B. Privet berries are POISONOUS.

Quince

LATIN NAME	Cydonia oblonga	POLARITY	Feminine
FAMILY	Rosaceae	ELEMENT	Water
ETYMOLOGY	ME, originally the plural	PLANET	Venus
	of quoyn, coyn or cooin,	DEITY	Dionysos, Venus
	from Latin cotoneum, a		
	variation of cydoneum, 'of		
	Cydonia' (a town in Crete)		

MAGICAL USES

Quince seeds are carried to protect against evil, physical harm, and accidents. Roman bridal couples shared a quince to ensure conjugal happiness. Eating quinces is said to ensure fidelity. If a pregnant woman eats a quince it is said to make the baby ingenious.

MEDICINAL USES

According to Culpeper, the quince-tree is ruled by Saturn. It is a mild astringent, used in small quantities for stomach upsets. The boiled seeds exude a soft mucilaginous substance which he used for sore mouths, throats, and breasts.

SYMBOLISM

A Greek symbol of fertility, the food of brides; the apple of Dionysos; sacred to Venus.

CULINARY USES

Quince jelly.

Rose

LATIN NAME	Rosa spp.	POLARITY	Feminine
FAMILY	Rosaceae	ELEMENT	Water
ETYMOLOGY	ME from OE rose from	PLANET	Venus
	Latin rosa	DEITY	Venus, Aphrodite

VARIETIES

There are 200-250 species of rose. Wild species include the dog rose (R. canina) and sweet briar or eglantine (R. rubiginosa or R. eglanteria). Modern cultivars are divided into four main groups, the first derived from the tea rose (R. odorata), the second from the floribundas; the other two groups are the climbers and the ramblers. Essential oil of rose is derived from the damask rose (R. damascena) and the cabbage rose (R. centifolia).

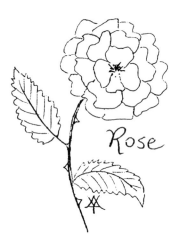

MAGICAL USES

Like many thorn-bearing shrubs, rose is used for psychic protection. A chaplet of roses is worn for love-magic, and a rose placed in a vase on the altar (with the thorns removed). Rose hips are worn as love-beads. Rosebud tea drunk before retiring to bed is said to give prophetic dreams. A spell to choose between admirers consists of taking one green rose leaf for each admirer and waiting to see which remains green the longest - the lover to whom this leaf was assigned will presumably remain ardent for the longest. (If on the other hand this refers to the longevity of your admirers, presumably you should choose the one which shrivels first if you want to collect on the will!) Rose petals and hips are used in healing spells. Roses planted in the garden are said to attract faeries, and to grow best when stolen. Rose petals are sprinkled around the house to calm personal stress and household disputes (alternatively, do the washing-up more often).

MEDICINAL USES

Rose-hips are rich in Vitamin C. In the Bach flower remedies, Dog Rose (R. canina) is used for those suffering from excessive apathy. Essential oil of rose cleanses and purges the vascular and digestive systems and soothes the nerves. It is useful in genito-urinary infections, and regulates menstruation. It is widely used as an aphrodisiac. The Mescalero Apaches treated gonorrhea with wild rosebud tea. Rose water reduces inflammation and is used as an eye-bath for conjunctivitis. Rose oil is good for reducing stress, is antiseptic, and good for the skin. A rose water poultice, applied to the temples, will relieve a headache. Rose hip syrup is an excellent source of vitamin C for children.

FOLKLORE

Sleeping Beauty's castle was surrounded by roses, their thorns making an impenetrable barrier. In German folklore, Sleeping Beauty is called Dornroschen (literally, thorn-rose, but usually translated as Briar Rose).

MYTHOLOGY

Aphrodite is said to have trodden on a white rose bush on her way to succour her wounded lover Adonis. The thorns tore her flesh, and her blood stained the rose red - thus the red rose was born. The red rose is sacred to Venus and Aphrodite, who rule over love, life, creation, fertility, creation, beauty, and virginity. According to Persian legend, rose oil was discovered at the wedding feast of the Princess Nour-Djihan and the Emperor Djihanguyr. A canal was dug and the water covered with rose-petals. The heat of the sun caused the rose oil to separate and float to the top; when the nature of this exudation was discovered, the production of rose oil followed soon after.

SYMBOLISM

Both Rosicrucians and Sufis use rose symbolism extensively. The Ruba'iyat of Omar Khayyam (a Sufi poem) uses the rose to symbolise the ephemeral nature of this life. Rosicrucianism originated in Germany in the 17th century; it is a blend of alchemy, Hermeticism, and neo-Platonism. In Rosicrucianism, the rose-cross contains the mystic rose as the wheel and the divine light of the universe and the cross as the temporal world of pain and sacrifice.

The rose is an ambivalent symbol: both heavenly perfection and earthly passion; Time and eternity; Life and Death; fertility and virginity. It symbolises perfection, the Pleroma, completion, the mystery of life, the heart, the unknown, beauty, grace, passion, happiness, and voluptuousness. Roses and wine represent seduction and sensuality. The rose and the heart denote unity. The evanescent rose symbolises death, mortality, and sorrow. The thorns of the rose represent pain, blood, and martyrdom. The rose as a funerary flower is eternal life, spring, and resurrection. The term 'sub rosa' denotes secrecy, discretion, and silence (a carving of the rose is hung in council chambers).

A golden rose represents perfection; a red rose, desire, passion, joy, beauty, consummation, the blood of Dionysos and Christ; a white rose, the flower of light, innocence, virginity, spiritual development, charm; a red and white rose, the union of fire and water, or the union of opposites; a blue rose, the attainment of the impossible; a four-petalled rose, the four-square division of the cosmos, the Four Elements. The Compass Rose or Rose of the Winds represents the cardinal directions and the winds.

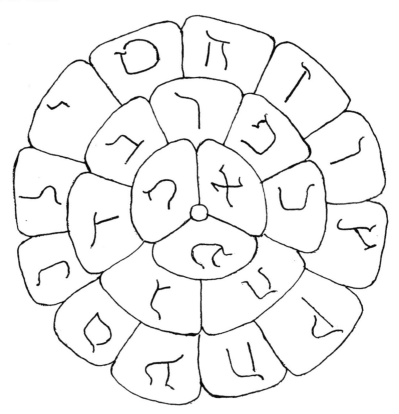

The Adept's Rose has 22 petals, one for each Hebrew letter, and relates to the paths of the Tree of Life; the inner ring of petals denotes Air, Fire, and Water, the middle ring is the seven planets, and the outer ring is the twelve signs of the Zodiac. To the Alchemists, the rose symbolised wisdom and the rebirth of the spiritual after the death of the temporal. In Egyptian symbolism the rose was an emblem of Isis and Osiris, symbolising pure love freed from carnal desire. To the Hebrews, the centre of the rose is the sun and the petals are the infinite and harmonious diversities of life. In Islam the rose is the blood of the Prophet, also his two sons. The Rose of Baghdad contains Truth and the three names of Allah; its first circle is the Law, its second the Path, its third Knowledge. In Christianity the white rose is the Virgin Mary; the red rose, charity and martyrdom; a garland of roses, heavenly bliss; a rose without thorns, the Virgin Mary as one without sin; and a golden rose, an emblem of Papal benediction. In the Wars of the Roses, the House of Lancaster had a red rose as its emblem, whilst the House of York had a white rose; the two cities still use a red and a white rose respectively as their emblems. When Henry VII of the House of Tudor came to the throne, he adopted the pink Tudor rose as his emblem, to symbolise both a reconciliation between Lancaster and York and the fact that he was descended from both Houses.

RHYMES & SONGS

"Gather ye rosebuds while ye may,
Old Time is still a-flying:
And this same flower that smiles to-day,
To-morrow will be dying."

(from Hesperides, 'To the Virgins, to Make Much of Time',
by Robert Herrick, 1591-1674)

"Here tulips bloom as they are told;
Unkempt about those hedges blows
An English unofficial rose."
(from 'Grantchester', by Rupert Brooke)

"Ring-a-ring-a-roses..." (Nursery rhyme,
referring to the red ring of buboes
occurring in bubonic plague)

" 'Tis the last rose of summer
Left blooming alone;
All her lovely companions
Are faded and gone."
(from 'Tis the Last Rose', Irish
Melodies, by Thomas Moore, 1779-1852)

"O my Love's like a red red rose
That's newly sprung in June"
(from 'My Love is like a Red Red Rose',
by Robert Burns, 1759-1796)

"I sometimes think that never blows so red
the Rose as where some buried Caesar bled."

(from 'The Ruba'iyat of Omar Khayyam',
Edward Fitzgerald, 1809-1883)

"Red Rose, proud Rose, sad Rose of all my days!"
(from "To the Rose upon the Rood of Time",
W. B. Yeats, 1865-1939)

"The rose distils a healing balm
the beating pulse of pain to calm."
(Anacreon)

CRAFT USES

Red rose petals can be used for dyeing. Rosaries were originally made of dried rosebuds (hence the name rosary), and the beads are still carved in the shape of rosebuds.

CULINARY USES

Rosehip tea; rose-petal wine; crystallised rose petals.

Rosewood

LATIN NAME   Aniba rosaeodora
FAMILY   Lauraceae

MEDICINAL USES

Oil of rosewood is used for coughs, colds, and fever; it stimulates the immune system; and it is used for nausea, headaches, tension, and stress.

CRAFT USES

The timber is used for building, carving, and French cabinet making.

Continued use of rosewood products is environmentally damaging, as huge areas of rainforest have been cut down to satisfy the demand for the timber, which is mainly used for the manufacture of chopsticks. Its use is not recommended for this reason.

Rowan or Mountain Ash

LATIN NAME	Sorbus aucuparia	POLARITY	Masculine
FAMILY	Rosaceae	ELEMENT	Air/Fire
FOLK NAMES	Berry Ash, Sheder (Lincs.);	PLANET	Mercury
	Quickbane, Ran-tree,	DEITIES	Odin, Thor
	Royne-tree, Roden-		
	Quicken-Royan, Sorb Apple,		
	Thor's Helper, Whitty,		
	Wild Ash, Wiggin, Wiggy,		
	Wiky, Witchen, Witchbane,		
	Witchwood, Wicken-tree.		
ETYMOLOGY	Norwegian rogn, raun, from	RUNES	Nyd/Nauthiz,
	Icelandic reynir		Calc
		OGHAM	Luis

VARIETIES

There are over 80 species in the genus Sorbus. A close relative of the Rowan is the Chinese Scarlet Rowan (S. discolor).

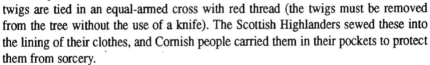

MAGICAL USES

Rowan trees are planted near the house to protect it from sorcery; the twigs are tied in an equal-armed cross with red thread (the twigs must be removed from the tree without the use of a knife). The Scottish Highlanders sewed these into the lining of their clothes, and Cornish people carried them in their pockets to protect them from sorcery.

Rowan rods are used as dowsing rods to find metal objects. In Lincolnshire the rowan is used to deflect the spells of malevolent male sorcerers. Rowan wands are placed over the door on quarter days to ensure good fortune; at Beltane they are combined with birch twigs to bring good fortune and fertility for the whole year, and placed over door lintels or newly-planted seed-beds. Rowan wood is said to increase psychic powers if carried. It can also be used to make wands. The leaves and berries are added to divination incenses; the berries and or bark are carried to aid recovery from illness, and added to healing and health sachets. Walking sticks of rowan are used by people roaming the woods and fields at night. Rowan wood was carried on ships to prevent storms and kept in the house to guard against lightning strikes; it is

163

placed on graves to ensure that the spirit of the deceased will have rest. Rowan trees growing near stone circles are reputed to be the most magically potent. Speer-posts, magically protective house-timbers inscribed with runes and magical patterns, were made of rowan-wood.

MYTHOLOGY

In Norse myth, it was a rowan tree which saved Thor from being swept away by a river in the Underworld - hence its folkname Thor's Helper.

SYMBOLISM

Wisdom; power against faeries and sorcery.

CRAFT USES

The timber is used to make tackle for water-mills, speer-posts (see MAGICAL USES) churn-staves, plough-pins, and pegs for tethering cattle. In the Middle Ages it ranked second to yew as a wood for making bows.

CULINARY USES

The berries are not palatable raw but can be used to make wine and jelly.

Great Sallow or Goat Willow

LATIN NAME	Salix caprea	POLARITY	Feminine
FAMILY	Salicaceae	ELEMENT	Water
FOLK NAME	Saugh, Pussy Willow	PLANET	Moon
		DEITY	Freyja
ETYMOLOGY	from Latin salix	RUNE	Lagu[z]
		OGHAM	Saille

VARIETIES

Common or Grey Sallow (S. cinerea)

MAGICAL USES

Pussy willow catkins are used to decorate churches in Spring in continuation of the pagan springtime custom of honouring Freyja, whose totem animal is the cat.

RHYMES & SONGS

"Down by the salley gardens my love and I did meet;
She passed the salley gardens with little snow-white feet.
She bid me take love easy, as the leaves grow on the tree;
But I, being young and foolish, with her would not agree."

(from "Down by the Salley Gardens", by W. B. Yeats, 1865-1939)

CRAFT USES
The wood is sometimes used for making clothes pegs.

Sandalwood

LATIN NAME	Santalum album	POLARITY	Feminine
FAMILY	Santalaceae	ELEMENT	Water
FOLK NAME	Sanders, Santal, White Saunders	PLANET	Moon, Uranus
ETYMOLOGY	from Sanskrit candala		

VARIETIES
The genus Santalum consists of about 25 species, native to S.E. Asia and the Pacific Islands.

MAGICAL USES
It is burned as an incense for protection, healing, and exorcism; mixed with lavender, it is used as an incense to conjure spirits. A wish is often written on a chip of sandalwood which is then burnt in censer or cauldron, whilst the practitioner visualises the wish. Sandalwood beads are worn for protection and to increase spiritual awareness. Powdered sandalwood is sprinkled to get rid of a negative atmosphere; it can also be used as an incense base. A mixture of sandalwood and crushed willow bark is burnt at the waning Moon to conjure spirits.

MEDICINAL USES
Essential oil of Sandalwood is good for sore throats, genito-urinary infections, and laryngitis. It has expectorant and anti-spasmodic effects.

CRAFT USES

The fragrant wood is used to make boxes and incense; the oil derived from it is used in perfumes, candles, and incense.

Wild Service

LATIN NAME	Sorbus torminalis	POLARITY	Masculine
FAMILY	Rosaceae	ELEMENT	Air
FOLK NAME	Chequers	PLANET	Saturn
		DEITY	Heimdall
ETYMOLOGY	from OE syrfe from	RUNE	Elhaz/Algiz
	Germanic surbhjon from		
	Latin sorbus		

VARIETIES

The Service Tree of Fontainebleau (S. x latifolia); The Service Tree (S. domestica)

MAGICAL USES

Service is a tree of protection against wild things; its wood can be used for wands and talismans.

MEDICINAL USES

According to Culpeper, the fruit (chequers) are restringent when unripe, and useful for all kinds of fluxes. The ripe fruit are still used for fevers accompanied by diarrhoea.

Spindle Tree

LATIN NAME	Euonymus europaeus	POLARITY	Masc./Fem.
FAMILY	Celastraceae	ELEMENTS	All
		PLANET	Venus
		DEITY	Frigga
ETYMOLOGY	from OE spinel from the	RUNE	Gar
	verb spinnan, to spin	OGHAM	Oir

VARIETIES
Broad-leaved Spindle Tree (E. latifolius), introduced to Britain in 186?; Japanese Spindle Tree (E. japonicus).

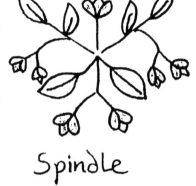

MEDICINAL USES
None - the berries are poisonous and a powerful emetic.

SYMBOLISM
Associated with the Cosmic Axis and the Heavenly Queen, Frigga in the Norse tradition, and hence the constellation of Orion, which is known as Frigg's Distaff in the Northern Tradition.

CRAFT USES
The wood was used for wool spindles, butchers' skewers, knitting needles, toothpicks, drawing charcoal, and small turnery. The powdered fruit is a powerful insecticide, and the boiled fruit can be used as a hair rinse. Red dye is obtained from the husks, and yellow dye from the pulp.

Norway or Common Spruce

LATIN NAME	Picea abies	POLARITY	Masculine
FAMILY	Pinaceae	ELEMENT	Fire/Air
		PLANET	Sun / Jupiter
FOLK NAME	Pitch-pine, Christmas-tree,	DEITY	Heimdall
	Tannenbaum		
ETYMOLOGY	from Pruce, an old word	RUNE	Daeg/Dagaz
	for Prussia		

VARIETIES

Sitka Spruce (P. sitchensis) from Sitka in Alaska, introduced to Britain in 1831.

MAGICAL USES

The Norway or Common Spruce is the Christmas-tree, a custom introduced to Britain by Prince Albert, husband of Queen Victoria. It originated in the German Yuletide custom (originally pagan) of venerating the sun-god in the form of an evergreen tree, whose vitality carried life on through the low ebb of the year at Midwinter. As the Yule tree, it is adorned with lights and silver spheres representing the stars and planets.

RHYMES & SONGS

"O Tannenbaum, O Tannenbaum
Wie schön sind deine Blätter"
(German Yule carol)

CRAFT USES

Spruce is used to make packing cases, paper pulp, ladder sides, interior construction, sleepers, joinery, furniture, tables, and certain stringed instruments. The timber is known as white deal. The tree also furnishes Burgundy pitch.

CULINARY USES

Spruce beer is made with the twigs and needles as flavouring and fermented with yeast and sugar.

Sycamore Fig

LATIN NAME	Ficus sycomorus	POLARITY	Feminine
FAMILY	Moraceae	ELEMENT	Air
FOLK NAME	Sycamine	PLANET	Venus
		DEITIES	Hathor, Artemis
ETYMOLOGY	from Hebrew sikmah		of Ephesus, Nut

MYTHOLOGY

The rites of Osiris in Egypt in the month of Khoiak culminated in the burial of an effigy of Osiris in a mulberry-wood coffin and the removal of the previous year's effigy to the boughs of a sycamore tree. Hathor was sometimes called the Lady of the Sycamore, for she sometimes hid in its foliage on the edge of the desert, and appeared to the dead with the bread and water of welcome.

SYMBOLISM

The Sycamore Fig is the Egyptian Tree of Life, sacred to Nut, goddess of the heavens, who was usually depicted on the inner lid of sarcophagi. The fruit of the sycamore fig yields a milky substance; hence it is sacred to the Mother Goddess Hathor, as the cow and nourishment, generation, fertility, and love. The tree is also connected with the many-breasted Artemis of Ephesus (who bears no relation to the Greek Artemis), a fertility goddess of Asia Minor, as the figs grow on the stock of the tree, and not on its branches.

Great Maple or Sycamore

LATIN NAME	Acer pseudoplatanus	POLARITY	Masculine
FAMILY	·Aceraceae ·	ELEMENT	Air
FOLK NAME	Plane (in Scotland)	PLANET	Jupiter
		DEITY	Heimdall
ETYMOLOGY	Latin sycaminus from	RUNE	Man[naz]
	Greek sukaminos from		
	Hebrew sikmah (mulberry		
	tree); maple from Celtic mapwl		

VARIETIES

The true sycamore is an eastern tree, Ficus sycomorus (Moraceae); it is not related to the Great Maple. Close relatives of the Great Maple are A. pseudoplatanus var.

169

purpureum (which has purple undersides to
its leaves) and A. pseudoplatanus var.
variegatum (with variegated leaves).

FOLKLORE
It makes good firewood.

MYTHOLOGY
The sycamore tree in Luke 17:6 was in fact a
sycamine or black mulberry tree (morus
nigra).

CRAFT USES
Turnery, furniture, domestic and agricultural
utensils, rollers, and parts of stringed instruments.

Sycamore
or
Great Maple

Tacamahac or Balsam Poplar

LATIN NAME   Calophyllum spp.
ETYMOLOGY   from Aztec tecomahiyac.

Yields a resinous gum known as tacamahac.

Tamarind

LATIN NAME	Tamarindus indica	POLARITY	Feminine
FAMILY	Leguminosae	ELEMENT	Water
ETYMOLOGY	from Arabic tamr-hindi, Indian date	PLANET	Saturn

MAGICAL USES
Tamarind fruit is carried to attract love. In Kampuchea (Cambodia), orchids growing
on tamarind trees were said to confer the gift of invulnerability.

MEDICINAL USES
Used in Indian folk-medicine.

MYTHOLOGY

In Burma, rain-spirits are said to dwell in the tamarind tree. The inhabitants of Monyo, a village in the Sagaing district of Upper Burma, chose the largest tamarind tree near the village and named it the abode of the spirit or nat who brings rain. Offerings of bread, coconuts, plantains, and fowls were made to the spirit, and it was beseeched to bring rain. Then libations were made, and three elderly women dressed in fine clothes and jewellery would sing the Rain Song.

CULINARY USES

Used in chutneys and curries.

Tamarisk

LATIN NAME	Tamarix spp.	POLARITY	Feminine
FAMILY	Tamaricaceae	ELEMENT	Water
		PLANET	Saturn
		DEITIES	Osiris, Anu, Apollo

VARIETIES

There are 90 species in the genus Tamarix.

MAGICAL USES

The use of tamarisk in exorcisms dates back at least 4000 years. A branch of tamarisk is held in the hand and the leaves are scattered about to ward off demons and evil. The branch is traditionally cut with a gold axe and a silver pruning knife. The smoke of burning tamarisk is said to drive away snakes. Tamarisk sticks were used for divination by the Chaldeans.

MYTHOLOGY

Tamarix mannifera, growing in the Middle East and Asia, exudes a sweet white edible substance known as manna when the stems are punctured by certain insects. It is probably this to which the book of Exodus refers; the Israelites, starving in the desert, were saved by manna from heaven.

In Sumero-Semitic myth it was sacred to Tammuz and Anu; it was a Tree of Life, and, with the date-palm, was said to have been created in heaven.

In Egyptian myth, when Seth killed Osiris, the coffin was washed out to sea by the Nile and across to Phoenicia, where it came to rest under a tamarisk tree,

171

which gave off a wonderful scent. Malcandre, King of Byblos in Phoenicia, gave orders that the tree should be cut down to be a prop for his palace roof. Isis heard of this marvel, and went to Phoenicia to find Osiris, whose body was still enclosed in the tree. For the Greeks, it was sacred to Apollo.

Tulip Tree

LATIN NAME	Liriodendron tulipifera	POLARITY	Feminine
FAMILY	Magnoliaceae	ELEMENT	Water
FOLK NAME	Saddle Tree (due to the shape of the leaves)	PLANET	Venus

MEDICINAL USES
An extract from the bark is used as a heart stimulant.

CRAFT USES
Flooring, furniture, carving, engineers' patterns, dairy utensils. The timber is referred to as canary wood or American whitewood in Britain.

172

Grape Vine

LATIN NAME	Vitis vinifera	POLARITY	Masculine
FAMILY	Vitis spp.	ELEMENT	Water
		PLANET	Venus
		DEITIES	Bacchus, Dionysos, Osiris, Tammuz, Apollo, Geshtinanna.
		OGHAM	Muin

VARIETIES
There are about 80 species of the genus Vitis; many of them are used in wine-making.

MYTHOLOGY
According to Egyptian myth, Osiris taught men the cultivation of the vine, hence it was sacred to him. In Sumero-Semitic mythology, it was sacred to Tammuz and Baal, and an attribute of Geshtinanna, goddess of the vine. To the Greeks and Romans, it was sacred to Bacchus, Dionysos, and Apollo. Priapus' statue was erected in vineyards to protect the vines and make them fruitful.

SYMBOLISM
Fecundity; life; a Tree of Life or Tree of Knowledge; sacred to Dying Gods. The fruitful vine represents fertility and passion; the wild vine denotes falseness and unfaithfulness. To the Buddhists, the vine is covetousness and desire (because it is a twining plant). In Christianity, Christ is the True Vine and the disciples are the branches (John 15); the vine also depicts the Church and the faithful. As a Tree of Life, with doves in its branches, it denotes souls at rest in Christ, and spiritual fruitfulness. A vine with corn represents the Eucharist (bread and wine). To the Hebrews, the vine represents the Chosen People; with the fig-tree it denotes peace and plenty.

RHYMES & SONGS

"Vine. I draw the blood from out the earth;
I store the sun for winter mirth."
(from "Tapestry Trees" by William Morris)

173

CULINARY USES
Wine-making; grapes are dried in various ways to make currants, raisins, and sultanas, which can be used for cakes, puddings, and sweet breads such as Peshwari Naan.

Walnut

LATIN NAME	Juglans regia	POLARITY	Masculine
FAMILY	Juglandaceae	ELEMENT	Earth/Fire
FOLK NAME	Tree of Evil, Walnoot	PLANET	Sun
		DEITY	Artemis
ETYMOLOGY	from OE walh-hnutu, meaning foreign nut		

VARIETIES
Including hickories, pecans, and wingnuts, there are about 50 species in the walnut family. The Black Walnut (J. nigra) was introduced to Europe from North America.

MAGICAL USES
Walnuts are carried to strengthen the heart and ward off rheumatic pains. They are said to attract lightning. The gift of a bag of walnuts is said to make all your wishes come true. Walnut leaves are worn on the hat to prevent sunstroke. A woman wishing to remain childless would, on her wedding day, place as many roasted walnuts in her bodice as the number of years for which she wanted to remain childless.

MEDICINAL USES
An infusion of the dried leaves can help eczema and cold sores; an infusion of powdered bark is said to be a laxative. Culpeper recommends walnut oil for falling hair, and the kernels beaten with rue and wine for inflammations of the ear. Edward Bach recommends walnut for those suffering for excessive enthusiasm for the ideas and goals of others; the remedy gives protection from outside influences and constancy.

MYTHOLOGY
Sacred to Artemis Karuatis. Caryatids were nymphs of the walnut tree.

SYMBOLISM
The nuts symbolise hidden wisdom, fertility, and longevity; they were served at Greek and Roman weddings to symbolise this. The tree symbolises strength in adversity, but also selfishness, because nothing grows beneath it.

CRAFT USES
The boiled green husks of the nuts yield a yellow dye; brown hair dye is obtainable from the leaves and outer shells. The timber is white in young trees and brown in mature ones. It takes a high polish and it is durable and strong; therefore it is ideal for cabinet work, furniture veneers, and gun stocks. The oil from the kernel of the nut can be used as a lamp oil and for making paint.

CULINARY USES
Green walnuts are pickled, preserved in vinegar, or made into a liqueur; ripe walnuts are an ingredient in cakes, biscuits, salads, stuffings, and sauces. Walnut oil is used as a salad dressing.

Wayfaring Tree

LATIN NAME	Viburnum lantana	POLARITY	Feminine
FAMILY	Caprifoliaceae	ELEMENT	Water
FOLK NAMES	Cotton Tree, Lithewort,	PLANET	Venus
	Mealy Tree, Whip Crop,	DEITY	Ing /Nerthus
	Twist Wood	RUNE	Rad/Raido

MAGICAL USES
A tree of protection, used for making travellers' talismans.

MEDICINAL USES
The leaves can be used to make a hair conditioner and a gargle for sore throats.

FOLKLORE
The tree was named the Wayfaring Tree by the herbalist John Gerard (1542-1612), because, he said, 'it is ever on the road'.

CRAFT USES

The twigs are used for making bird-lime. In Germany the young shoots were used in basket-making and for tying faggots and parcels, and the older shoots were used for making tobacco pipes. In Switzerland the berries were used to make ink. In England ploughboys twisted the stems into handles for whips, hence the names Whip Crop and Twist Wood. The leaves can be used to make a dark dye.

Whitebeam

LATIN NAME	Sorbus aria	POLARITY	Masculine
FAMILY	Rosaceae	ELEMENT	Air
FOLK NAMES	Hen-apple, Bean Tree,	PLANET	Mercury /Venus
	Lot-tree, Cumberland		
	Hawthorn, Hoar Withy,		
	Sea Owler, Wild Cowbin.		

VARIETIES

There are several cultivars of Whitebeam. Swedish Whitebeam (S. intermedia) may be a cross between the Whitebeam and the Rowan (S. aucuparia).

CRAFT USES

The timber is used for tool handles, bobbins, mallet-heads, small turnery, cabinet-work, furniture, and plywood.

CULINARY USES

The fruit (known as the chess apple in Lancashire and Cumbria) is edible after being touched by frost, and is sometimes used to make jam and wine.

Willow

LATIN NAME	Salix spp.	POLARITY	Feminine
FAMILY	Salicaceae	ELEMENT	Water
FOLKNAME	Witches' Aspirin	PLANET	Moon
		DEITIES	Kuan Yin, Artemis, Hecate, Persephone
ETYMOLOGY	from OE welig	RUNE	Lagu[z]
		OGHAM	Saille

VARIETIES
Grey Sallow or Common Willow (S. cinerea); White Willow (S. alba); Crack Willow (S. fragilis).

MAGICAL USES
The willow tree is symbolic of purification and rebirth; staves cut from it will put forth roots and become new trees. It is used in the ceremony of beating the

bounds (defining the parish boundary), an annual springtime ritual of purification. In Japan, mistletoe growing on the willow is given to barren women who wish to bear children. Willow trees are sometimes used in a similar manner to ash (q.v.) for the cure of rickets; the rite is usually performed widdershins (anti-clockwise). Willow leaves are carried to attract love. The wood is used to make wands for lunar magic. A spell to find out if one will be married in the next year is to throw one's shoe into a willow tree on New Year's Eve, and if it has not lodged there after nine throws one will not be married in the next year (there is no mention of how one is supposed to retrieve the shoe if it does lodge there - being nine parts cut and in the dark does not seem like a good time to start climbing trees). The custom of knocking on wood possibly has its origin in the custom of knocking on a willow tree to avert evil. The leaves, bark, and wood are used in healing spells. The besom of a witch's broom is traditionally bound on with willow thongs. Sandalwood mixed with crushed willow bark and burnt during the waning Moon is used to conjure spirits.

177

Willow

MEDICINAL USES

Salicylic acid, the active ingredient of aspirin, is derived from the willow tree. In the Bach flower remedies, willow is used for those who are embittered by misfortune or adversity and find it difficult to accept.

FOLKLORE

"The willow will buy the horse before the oak will buy the saddle." (Country saying - refers to the fact that the willow is faster-growing than the oak.)

Willow is used in the Festival of Green George amongst the Rumanian Gypsies. A young willow is cut down on the eve of the festival, which is celebrated on Easter Monday or St. George's Day (23rd April), and pregnant women lay garments under the tree. If a leaf falls on their garment, they will have an easy delivery.

MYTHOLOGY

In China, the willow is sacred to Kuan Yin, the bodhisattva of compassion, who sprinkles the waters of life with a willow-branch. In Europe, it symbolises death as a force for change and new growth; also unrequited love. According to Robert Graves, the wearing of willow in the hat as a sign of the rejected lover seems to have originated as a charm against the jealousy of the Moon Goddess. The willow is sacred to the Moon, which symbolises fickle and changeable emotions and illusion (amongst other things). In Japanese legend, the spine of the first man was made from willow.

SYMBOLISM

To the Chinese, willow symbolises spring, femininity, meekness, grace, charm, artistic ability, parting, and the yin or lunar qualities. In Graeco-Roman symbolism it is an emblem of Artemis and sacred to Europa (see PLANE). In Hebraic symbolism it is mourning and the weeping of the exiled tribes of Israel by the willows of Babylon. There is a day of willows in the Feast of Tabernacles (Succoth). To the Japanese, it represents patience and perseverance, and is especially sacred among the Ainu. In Sumero-Semitic symbolism it was an emblem of Tammuz, representing triumph, rejoicing, and happiness; and it was the cosmic tree of the Akkadians, sacred to the Akkadian Zeus. The withy is an emblem of Artemis and childbirth. To the Taoists, the willow is strength in weakness, contrasted with the pine or the oak, which resist the storm and are broken by it, whereas the willow bends, giving way to the storm, springs back after it has passed, and thus survives.

CRAFT USES

Willow is a resilient wood, good for fencing, thatching spars, cricket bats, wattles, and sticks for beating the bounds (see MAGICAL USES).

RHYMES & SONGS

"All Around My Hat" (Anon);

"To the Willow-tree" (Robert Herrick, 1591-1674)

"All a green willow, willow;
All a green willow is my garland."
(from "The Green Willow" by John Heywood,1497-1580)

To the Willow-tree

Thou art to all lost love the best,
  The only true plant found,
Wherewith young men and maids distrest,
  And left of love, are crown'd.

When once the lover's rose is dead,
  Or laid aside forlorn:
Then willow-garlands 'bout the head
  Bedew'd with tears are worn.

When with neglect, the lovers' bane,
  Poor maids rewarded be
For their love lost, their only gain
  Is but a wreath from thee.

And underneath thy cooling shade,
  When weary of the light,
The love-spent youth and love-sick maid
  Come to weep out the night.

Robert Herrick (1591-1674)

180

All around my hat

My love she was fair and my love she was kind
And cruel the judge and jury that sentenced her away
For thieving was a thing that she never was inclined to
They sent my love across the sea ten thousand miles away.

All around my hat I will wear the green willow
All around my hat for a twelvemonth and a day
And if anyone should ask me the reason for my wearing it
I'll tell them my own true love is ten thousand miles away.

I bought my love a golden ring to wear upon her finger
A token of our own true love and to remember me
And when she returns again we'll never more be parted
We'll marry and be happy for ever and a day.

Seven, seven long years my love and I are parted
Seven, seven long years my love is bound to stay
Seven long years I'll love my love and never be false-hearted
And never sigh or sorrow while she's far, far away.

Some young men there are who are preciously deceitful
A-coaxing of the fair young maids they mean to lead astray
As soon as they deceive them, so cruelly they leave them
I'll love my love forever though she's far, far away.

(Anon.)

Willow

Witch-hazel

LATIN NAME	Hamamelis virginica	POLARITY	Masculine
FAMILY	Hamamelidaceae	ELEMENT	Fire
FOLK NAMES	Snapping Hazelnut, Spotted	PLANET	Sun
	Alder, Winterbloom	RUNE	Stan

VARIETIES
There are six species in the Hamamelidaceae family.

MAGICAL USES
Witch hazel is used to make divining rods. The bark and twigs are used to protect against evil influences. Witch hazel is carried to help mend a broken heart and cool the passions. It is also used to protect against faeries, sorcery, and evil spirits. It can also be used in divination.

MEDICINAL USES
The oil of witch hazel is used to allay bleeding and reduce the swelling of bruises. Diluted it is used as an eye wash.

CRAFT USES
The oil of witch hazel is used in perfumery.

Yew

LATIN NAME	Taxus baccata	POLARITY	Feminine
FAMILY	Taxaceae	ELEMENT	Earth
		PLANET	Saturn
		DEITY	Hecate
ETYMOLOGY	from OE iw, eow, from	RUNES	Eolh/Eihwaz,
	Germanic (cf. Old French		Yr
	ivo)	OGHAM	Ioh

VARIETIES
Irish Yew (T. baccata 'Fastigiata'); Westfelton Yew (T. baccata 'Dovastoniana')

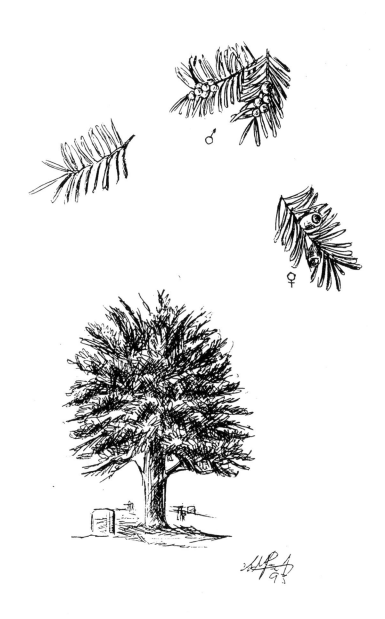

Yew

MAGICAL USES

Associated with eternal life, yew was planted in places of interment, and is common in British churchyards. In hot weather it gives off a resinous vapour which shamans inhaled to gain visions. Yew wood was regarded as especially magical by the Gaels; the Gaelic White Wand was traditionally made of yew. White is the colour of the Earth Goddess.

Yews

MEDICINAL USES

None - yew is POISONOUS, especially the dried leaves.

MYTHOLOGY

The Norse god Uller, god of archery and winter, lived in a sacred yew grove called Ydalir, valley of the yews.

SYMBOLISM

Funerary, mourning, sadness. A Celtic and Christian tree of immortality.

RHYMES & SONGS

"Beech-logs for winter-time
Yew-logs as well..." (Dartmoor folk song)

"Yew. Dark down the windy dale I grow
The father of the fateful Bow."
(from "Tapestry Trees" by William Morris)

"The yew-tree points up. It has a Gothic shape.
The eyes lift after it and find the moon.
....
And the message of the yew tree is blackness - blackness and silence."
(from "The Moon and the Yew Tree" by Sylvia Plath)

CRAFT USES

Yew wood was used in the Middle Ages for bow-making. Yews are excellent for hedging and topiary, but should not be planted near grazing animals. The timber is good for fence-posts, furniture, and small tools; it is extremely hard.

184

Ylang-ylang

LATIN NAME	Cananga odorata	POLARITY	Feminine
FAMILY	Anonaceae	ELEMENT	Water
		PLANET	Venus
ETYMOLOGY	from Chinese "Flower of flowers"		

MEDICINAL USES
Ylang-ylang essential oil is aphrodisiac, relaxing, and reduces stress and anxiety. It is good for intestinal infections due to its antiseptic qualities, and it is good for oily skin when used in a facial massage. It is also antidepressant.

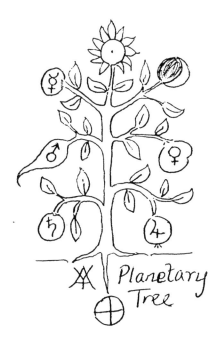

185

APPENDIX A:
LIST OF GROUPS CONCERNED FOR THE ENVIRONMENT

Alarm UK:

The Alliance Against Road-building (promotes radical grass-roots campaigning). New members receive information pack on campaigning. Membership costs £10 p.a. and includes the newsletter Alarm Bells.

Alarm UK, 13 Stockwell Road, LONDON, SW9 9AU. (071 737 6641)

CPRE:

Council for the Protection of Rural England (a long-standing pressure group for a variety of countryside issues including quarrying and road-building.

CPRE, Warwick House, 25 Buckingham Palace Road, LONDON, SW1W 0PP.

Friends of the Earth:

all environmental issues. For details, contact your local FoE group, or write to FoE, 26-28 Underwood Street, LONDON, N1 7JQ.

Transport 2000

(promotes use of alternative eco-friendly forms of transport).

Transport 2000, 3rd floor, Walkden House, 10 Melton Street, LONDON, NW1 2EJ. (071 388 8386)

Earth First!

(Radical eco-activists - contact your local group)

DRAGON

(eco-pagan action group) c/o Adrian Harris, 3 Sanford Walk, New Cross, LONDON, SE14 6NB.

Assyro-Babylonian
Moon Tree

Babylonian
Moon-Tree

Druidic
mistletoe
Sigil

APPENDIX B:
TREE FAMILIES

Aceraceae: Common or Field Maple (Acer campestre L.)
Sycamore or great Maple (Acer pseudoplatanus L.)

Anacardiaceae: Cashew (Anacardium occidentale)
Pepper tree (Schinus molle)
Mastic (Pistacia lentiscus)
Pistachio (Pistacia vera)

Annonaceae: Cananga (Cananga odorata var. macrophylla)
Ylang-ylang (Cananga odorata var. genuina)

Aquifoliaceae: Holly (Ilex aquifolium)

Arialaceae: Ivy (Hedera helix)

Bambusidae: Bamboo (Bambusa vulgaris)

Betulaceae: Common or Black Alder (Alnus glutinosa)
Silver Birch (Betula pendula)
Hazel or Cobnut (Corylus avellana L.)
Common Hornbeam (Carpinus betulus)
Sweet or Cherry Birch (Betula lenta)

Burseraceae: Frankincense (Boswellia carteri)
Linaloe or Copal Limon (Bursera glabrifolia)
Myrrh (Commiphora myrrha)
Opoponax (Commiphora erythraea)

Buxaceae: Common Box (Buxus sempervirens L.)

Caesalpina: Brazil Nut (Bertholletia excelsa)

Caprifoliaceae: Elder or Bourtree (Sambucus nigra L.)
Guelder Rose (Viburnum opulus L.)
Wayfaring Tree (Viburnum lantana L.)

Caricaceae: Papaya (Carica papaya)

Celastraceae: Spindle Tree (Euonymus europaeus L.)

Cornaceae: Dogwood or Cornel (Cornus sanguinea L.)

Cupressaceae: Monterey Cypress (Cupressus macrocarpa)
Common Juniper (Juniperus communis L.)

Dipterocarpaceae: Borneo Camphor (Dryobalanops aromatica)

Ebenaceae: Persimmon (Diospyros spp.)

Eleagnaceae: Sea or Sallow Buckthorn (Hippophae rhamnoides L.)

Ericaceae: Azalea (Azalea spp.)
Heather (Erica spp.)

Euphorbiaceae: Cascarilla (Croton eluteria)

Fagaceae: European Beech (Fagus sylvatica L.)
Sweet or Spanish Chestnut (Castanea sativa)
Common or Pedunculate Oak (Quercus robur L.)
Turkey Oak (Quercus cerris L.)
Cork Oak (Quercus suber L.)
American Red Oak (Quercus rubra)
Pin Oak (Quercus palustris)
Scarlet Oak (Quercus coccinea)
Holm or Evergreen Oak (Quercus ilex)

Hamamelidaceae: Witch Hazel (Hamamelis spp.)

Hippocastanaceae:White or Common Horse Chestnut
(Aesculus hippocastanum L.)

Juglandaceae: Common Walnut (Juglans regia)
Black Walnut (Juglans nigra)
Hickory (Carya spp.)
Wingnut (Pterocarya spp.)
Pecan (Carya illinoensis)

Lauraceae: Bay Laurel (Laurus nobilis)
Camphor (Cinnamonum camphora)
Cassia (Cinnamomum cassia)

Cinnamon (Cinnamomum zeylanicum)
Rosewood (Aniba rosaeodora)

Leguminosae: Gorse, Furze, or Whin (Ulex europaeus L.)
Broom (Cytisus scoparius)
Western Gorse (Ulex gallii)
Dwarf Gorse (Ulex minor)
Common Laburnum or Golden Rain (Laburnum anagyroides)
False Acacia (Robinia pseudoacacia - LOTOIDAE)
Acacia (Acacia spp.)
Tamarind (Tamarindus indica)
Copaiba Balsam (Copaifera officinalis)
Peru Balsam (Myroxylon balsamum var. pereirae)
Tolu Balsam (Myroxylon balsamum var. balsamum)

Loranthaceae: Mistletoe (Viscum album)

Magnoliaceae: Magnolia (Magnolia spp.)
Tulip Tree (Liriodendron tulipifera L.)

Mimosaceae: Mimosa or Black Sydney Wattle (Acacia dealbata)

Moraceae: Fig (Ficus carica L.)
Common Mulberry (Morus nigra L.)
Banyan (Ficus benghalesis)
Bo Tree (Ficus religiosa)

Musaceae: Banana (Musa sapientum)

Myristicaceae: Nutmeg (Myristica fragrans)

Myrtaceae: Eucalyptus (Eucalyptus spp.)
Ti tree (Melaleuca alternifolia)
West Indian Bay or Bay Rum tree (Pimenta racemosa)
Cajeput (Melaleuca cajeputi)
Clove (Syzygium aromaticum)
Niaouli (Melaleuca viridiflora)

Oleaceae: Common Ash (Fraxinus excelsior L.)
Common Privet (Ligustrum vulgare L.)
Oval-leaved Privet (Ligustrum ovalifolium)
Shining Privet (Ligustrum lucidum)

Jasmine (Jasminum spp.)
Olive (Olea europaea)

Palmae:	Coconut (Cocos nucifera) Date Palm (Phoenix dactilyfera)

Pinaceae:

Canadian Balsam (Abies balsamea)
Noble Fir (Abies procera)
[Green] Douglas Fir (Pseudotsuga menziesii)
Western Hemlock (Tsuga heterophylla)
Eastern Hemlock (Tsuga canadensis)
Mountain Hemlock (Tsuga mertensiana)
Norway or Common Spruce (Picea abies)
Sitka Spruce (Picea sitchensis)
Serbian Spruce (Picea omorika)
European Larch (Larix decidua)
Cedar of Lebanon (Cedrus libani)
Scots Pine (Pinus sylvestris L.)
Maritime or Cluster Pine (Pinus pinaster)
Coastal Lodgepole or Beach Pine (Pinus contorta)
Norfolk Island Pine (Auricaria excelsa)

Platanaceae:

London Plane (Platanus x hispanica)
Oriental Plane (Platanus orientalis)
Western Plane (Platanus occidentalis)

Punicaceae:

Pomegranate (Punica granatum)

Rhamnaceae:

Alder Buckthorn (Frangula alnus)
Mediterranean Buckthorn (Rhamnus alaternus)
Purging Buckthorn (Rhamnus catharticus L.)

Rosaceae:

Almond (Prunus dulcis)
Bitter Almond (P. dulcis var. amara)
Crab Apple (Malus sylvestris)
Apricot (Prunus armeniaca)
Blackthorn (Prunus spinosa)
Bramble (Rubus fruticosa)
Wild Cherry (Prunus avium)
Damson (Prunus institia)
Hawthorn (Crataegus monogyna)
Peach (Prunus persica)

Pear (Pyrus communis)
Plum (Prunus domesticus)
Quince (Cydonia oblonga)
Rose (Rosa spp.)
Rowan (Sorbus aucuparia)
Service (Sorbus torminalis)
Whitebeam (Sorbus aria)

Rutaceae:
Seville Orange or Neroli (Citrus aurantium)
Sweet Orange (Citrus sinensis)
Tangerine (Citrus reticulata)
Temple Orange - hybrid of Sweet Orange and Tangerine
Grapefruit (Citrus paradisi)
Lemon (Citrus limon)
Lime (Citrus aurantifolia)
Citron (Citrus medica)
Bergamot (Citrus bergamia)

Salicaceae:
Aspen (Populus tremula L.)
Common Osier (Salix viminalis L.)
White Poplar (Populus alba)
Great Sallow or Goat Willow (Salix caprea L.)
Crack Willow (Salix fragilis L.)
Grey Poplar (Populus canescens)
Black Poplar (Populus nigra var. betulifolia)

Styraceae:
Benzoin (Styrax benzoin)

Tamaricaceae:
Tamarisk (Tamarix spp.)

Taxaceae:
Yew (Taxus baccata)

Tiliaceae:
Common Lime or Linden (Tilia x vulgaris Hayne)
Small-leaved Lime (Tilia cordata)
Large-leaved Lime (Tilia platyphyllos)

Ulmaceae:
Wych or Scots Elm (Ulmus glabra)
Common, English, or Small-leaved Elm (Ulmus procera)

Zygophyllaceae: Guaiac wood (Bulnesia sarmienti)

Appendix C
Dartmoor Folk Song

Oak-logs will warm you well,
That are old and dry;
Logs of pine will sweetly smell
But the sparks will fly.
Birch-logs will burn too fast,
Chestnut scarce at all;
Hawthorn-logs are good to last -
Catch them in the fall.
Holly-logs will burn like wax,
You may burn them green;
Elm-logs like to smouldering flax,
No flame to be seen.
Beech-logs for winter-time,
Yew-logs as well;
Green elder-logs it is a crime
For any man to sell.
Pear-logs and apple-logs,
they will scent your room,
Cherry-logs across the dogs
Smell like flower of the broom.
Ash-logs, smooth and grey,
Burn them green or old,
Buy up all that come your way -
Worth their weight in gold.

BIBLIOGRAPHY

I have only given the year of publication in cases where it is possible that the work is no longer in print, or the date is relevant for comparison of other similar works, or where the work is an article.

BOOKS

Nicholas Culpeper,	Culpeper's Herbal (Foulsham Books)
	Concise Oxford Dictionary (OUP)
	The Macmillan Encyclopedia (Macmillan)
	New Larousse Encyclopedia of Mythology (Larousse)
Nigel Pennick,	Practical Magic in the Northern Tradition (Aquarius Books)
Nigel Pennick,	The Secret Lore of Runes and Other Ancient Alphabets (Rider)
Freya Aswynn,	Leaves of Yggdrasil (Llewellyn)
Alan Fairhurst and Eric Soothill,	Trees of the Countryside: a Recognition Guide, (Blandford)
William Shakespeare,	The Complete Works (plays, poems, and sonnets)
E. V. Lucas,	The Open Road (Methuen, 1914)
R. K. Gordon,	Anglo-Saxon Poetry (Dent & Dutton, Everyman, 1950)
Robin Skelton and Margaret Blackwood,	Earth, Air, Fire, and Water: Pre-Christian and Pagan Elements in British Songs, Rhymes, and Ballads (Arkana)
Lesley Bremness,	The Complete Book of Herbs (RK)
M. Esther Harding,	Woman's Mysteries, Ancient and Modern (Shambhala)
Sir A. Quiller-Couch (ed.),	The Oxford Book of English Verse (OUP, 1918)
W. B. Yeats (ed.),	The Oxford book of Modern Verse, 1892-1935, (OUP, 1935?)
Philip Larkin (ed.),	The Oxford Book of Twentieth Century English Verse (OUP, 1973, reprinted 1988)
	Encyclopedia of Garden Plants and Flowers (Reader's Digest)
H. de Lubac,	Aspects of Buddhism (Sheed & Ward, 1953)
J. C. Cooper,	An Illustrated Encyclopedia of Traditional Symbols (Thames and Hudson)
Z'ev ben Shimon Halevi,	Kabbalah: Tradition of Hidden Knowledge (Mandala)
Robert Tisserand,	The Art of Aromatherapy (C. W. Daniel)
Julia Lawless,	The Encyclopedia of Essential Oils (Element)

Bibliography

Scott Cunningham,	Cunningham's Encyclopedia of Magical Herbs (Llewellyn)
Aleister Crowley,	777
Dr. Edward Bach,	The Twelve Healers
Evan John Jones,	Witchcraft: A Tradition Renewed (Hale)
David N. Pegler,	The Mitchell Beazley Pocket Guide to Mushrooms and Toadstools (Mitchell Beazley)
Robin Page,	Weather Forecasting the Country Way (Penguin)
Janet and Stewart Farrar,	The Witches' God: Lord of the Dance (Hale)
Janet and Stewart Farrar,	The Witches' Goddess: The feminine principle of divinity (Hale)
J. G. Frazer,	The Golden Bough (abridged edn., Macmillan)
Robert Graves,	The White Goddess (Faber & Faber)
Kevin Crossley-Holland,	The Norse Myths (Penguin)
J. Mayo,	Astrology (Teach Yourself Books)
Edward Fitzgerald,	The Ruba'iyat of Omar Khayyam
W. B. Yeats,	Selected Poetry (ed. A. Norman Jeffares; Papermac)
Brian Bates,	The Way of Wyrd (Arrow)
Dion Fortune,	The Sea Priestess (Aquarius)
E. M. Forster,	Howard's End (Penguin)
Sylvia Plath,	Ariel (Faber & Faber)
Paul Kay	An Idiot's Guide to Incense

ARTICLES

Soror Rachel,	Notes on the Oak (OTO Newsletter, Vol. III no. 9, August 1979)
Julie Pembridge	(nee Frusher), Herbcraft Part 15: Mistletoe and Holly (The Wiccan, Imbolc 1993)
Bernard King,	The Hyperborean Horses (Talking Stick, Issue XI, Summer 1993)
	The Woman and Tree Motif in Prakrit and Sanskrit Texts (Journal of Asiatic Society, Letters and Science, Vol. XXIII, No. 1, 1957)

Index

195

Index

Index

A selection of other titles from Capall Bann:

Available through your local bookshop, or direct from Capall Bann, Freshfields, Chieveley, Berks.

West Country Wicca - A Journal of the Old Religion By Rhiannon Ryall

This book is a valuable and enjoyable contribution to contemporary Wicca. It is a simple account of the Old Religion. The portrayal of Wicca in the olden days is at once charming and deeply religious, combining joy, simplicity and reverence. The wisdom emanating from country folk who live close to Nature shines forth from every page - a wisdom which can add depth and colour to our present day understanding of the Craft. Without placing more value on her way than ours, Rhiannon provides us with a direct path back to the Old Religion in the British Isles. *This is how it was*, she tells us. *This is the way I remember it.* Both the content of what she remembers and the form in which she tells us, are straightforward, homespun and thoroughly unaffected.

"West Country Wicca is a real gem - it is the best book on witchcraft I have ever seen! Thank you Rhiannon Ryall for sharing your path with us." - Marion Weinstein

ISBN Number   1 89830 702 4   Price £7.95

Pathworking 2nd Ed. By Pete Jennings & Pete Sawyer

A complete and easy to understand guide from two experienced fieldworkers. A pathworking is, very simply, a guided meditational exercise, it is sometimes referred to as 'channelling' or 'questing'. It is used for many different aims, from raising consciousness to healing rituals You don't have to possess particular beliefs or large sums of money to benefit from it and it can be conducted within a group or solo at time intervals to suit you. This book teaches you how to alter your conscious state, deal with stress, search for esoteric knowledge or simply have fun and relax. It starts with a clear explanation of the theory of pathworking and shows in simple and concise terms what it is about and how to achieve results, then goes on to more advanced paths and how to develop your own, it also contains over 30 detailed and explained pathworkings. Highly practical advice and information is given on how to establish and manage your own group. No previous experience is assumed, so the book will be beneficial to new and experienced readers alike. If you have ever wondered how to do it or what is behind it, all is revealed!

'Full of ideas and highly recommended' *The Wiccan*

'Sound magical, technical and practical advice on the subject .... It really is a must for anyone who wants to have a go...' *Deosil Dance*

'down to earth, easy to read and suitable for group workings... ' *Odinshof Bulletin*

'Experienced people producing a book of decent, graduated pathworkings with proper instructions has been needed for some time and here it is so go out and buy it' *Gates of Annwn*

ISBN Number   1 898307 00 8   Price £7.95

Angels & Goddesses - Celtic Paganism & Christianity
by Michael Howard

The purpose of this book is threefold. Firstly it traces the history and development of Celtic Paganism and Celtic Christianity specifically in Wales, but also in relation to the rest of the British Isles including Ireland, during the period from the Iron Age, through the Roman occupation, the Dark Ages, the Middle Ages and up to the present day. The second theme of the book is a study of the transition between the old pagan religions and Christianity and how the early Church, especially in the Celtic counmtries, both struggled with and later absorbed the earlier forms of spirituality it encountered. This can be clearly seen in the history of early Christianinty in Roman Britain and in the later development of Celtic Christianity when pagan and Christian beliefs co-existed, albeit in an uneasy and sometimes violent relationship.

The book also deals with the way in which the Roman Catholic version of Christianity arrived in south-east England and the end of the 6th centuy, when the Pope sent St. Augustine on his famous mission to convert the pagan Saxons, and how this affected the Celtic Church.. It discusses how the Roman Church suppressed Celtic Christianity and the effect this was to have on the history and theology of the Church during the later Middle Ages. The influence of Celtic Chhristianity on the Arthurian legends and the Grail romances is explored as well as surviving traditions of Celtic bardism in the medieval period. The conclusion on the book covers the interest in Celtic Christianity today and how, despite attempts to eradicate it from the pages of clerical history, its ideas and ideals have managed to survive and are now influencing New age concepts and are relevent to the critical debate about the future of the modem chrurch.

ISBN 1-898307-03-2   Price £9.95

Auguries & Omens - The Magical Lore of Birds
By Yvonne Aburrow

This is a truly unique book covering the mythology, folklore and legends of birds. Associated rhymes and songs are also included together with the esoteric correspondences - polarity, planet, deity etc. There is a short history of bird lore, its purpose and applications . The text is profusely illustrated with line drawings. This book is packed with fascinating information which will not only appeal to readers interested in folklore, but to bird lovers everywhere.

Publication date   February 1994

The Sacred Grove - The Mysteries of the Tree
By Yvonne Aburrow

The practical use sequel to The Enchanted Forest. This book consists of pathworkings, seasonal rituals and practical guidance on the use of trees in magic, giving a new perspective on the cycle of seasonal festivals.

Publication date

The Inner Space Work Book - Developing Counselling & Magickal Skills Through the Tarot
By Cat Summers & Julian Vayne

Not just another book on tarot layout and readings. This is a detailed, practical book on psychic and personal development using the Tarot, pathworkings and meditations. The Inner Space Work Book provides a framework for developing your psychic and magickal abilities; exploring techniques as varied as shamanism, bodymind skills and ritual, through the medium of the tarot. There are two interwoven pathways through the text. One concentrates on the development of psychic sensitivity, divination and counselling, as well as discussing their ethics and practical application. The second pathway leads the student deeper into the realm of Inner Space, exploring the Self through meditation, pathworking, physical exercises and ritual. Both paths weave together to provide the student with a firm grounding in many aspects of the esoteric.

Together, the pathways in The Inner Space Work Book, form a 'user friendly' system for unlocking all your latent magickal talents.

ISBN 1 898307 13 X   Price £9.95

Earth Magic - A Seasonal Guide
By Margaret McArthur   Edited by Julia Day

This book gives an introduction to the real feeling of The Old Religion. The author has concentrated on giving information on this nature based religion in a simple, straightforward manner. The book starts with a background and introduction section, then goes on to describe the seasons of the year and their associated festivals, Earth Magic and the elements used in it. Food has always been an important part of the major festivals, Margaret is renowned for her culinary as well as her psychic skills and passes on many traditional recipes in this book together with their meanings and associations .

Margaret McArthur describes herself as a 'hedge witch' and has been involved in a traditional path of the Old Religion for many years. She is well known and highly respected by followers of many different pagan paths.

Many books have been written about the Old Religion, but most concentrate on giving out set rituals and wordings. This book is different in that it concentrates on encouraging readers to get the 'feel' for the elements, plants and other parts of nature and to work with them rather than try to subdue them. This is an important book for the 90's and will help many seekers find a simple, satisfying path of beliefs.

Illustrations by Gill Bent.

ISBN Number   1 898307 016   Price £9.95

The Mysteries of the Runes By Michael Howard

Michael Howard is internationally known as a leading expert on the runes. The book commences by defining the word 'rune', following the historical development of the runes from earlier Neolithic and Bronze Age alphabets and symbols and their connection with other magical and mystical symbols including the swastika, sunwheel, equal-armed cross etc. Historical references to the runes and their use in divination by Germanic tribes and the Saxons together with the Viking use of the runes in Dark Age England are also covered. The Norse god Odin is discussed, as the shaman-god of the runes together with his associated myths, legends and folklore, the Wild Hunt, the Valkyries and his connections with the Roman god Mercury, the Egyptian god Thoth, Jesus and the Odinic mysteries. The section ends describing the magical uses of the runes, their use in divination with examples of their everyday use. Fascinating information is included on the runes discovered during archaelogical excavations, rune masters and mistresses, the bog sacrifices of Scandanavia and the training of the rune master, both ancient and modern.

The second section explains the symbolism of the runes and their place in pre-Christian society - the pagan world view. Detailed descriptions of each of the eight runes of Freya's Aett, Haegl's Aett and Tyr's Aett are given with divinity, religious symbolism and spiritual meanings etc based on The Anglo Saxon Rune Poem. The section finishes with details on how to make your own set of runes, how to cast the runes for divination with examples of rune readings with suggested layouts. This section also covers the use of rune magic.

The final section covers Bronze Age Scandanavia and its religious belief systems; the gods and goddess of the Aesir and Vanir, their myths and legends and the seasonal cycle of festivals in the Northern Tradition. The theories regarding Hyperborea and the 'Atlantis of the North' are explored together with the concept of duality in Indo-European religion religion - the Web of Wyrd and the Norns, Saxon/Norse paganism and traditional witchcraft.

ISBN Number   1-898307-07-0   Price £8.95

The Call of the Horned Piper by Nigel Aldcroft Jackson

This book originated as a series of articles, later much expanded, covering the symbolism, archetypes and myths of the Traditional Craft (or Old Religion) in the British Isles and Europe. The first section of the book explores the inner symbology and mythopoetics of the old Witchraft religion, whilst the second part gives a practical treatment of the sacred sabbatic cycle, the working tools, incantations, spells and pathworking. There are also sections on spirit lines, knots and thread lore and ancestral faery teachings. Extensively illustrated with the author's original artwork. This is a radical and fresh re-appraisal of authentic witch-lore which may provide a working alternative to current mainstream trends in Wicca.

ISBN Number   1-898307-09-1   Price £8.95

Capall Bann Publishing is owned and run by people with experience and beliefs in the fields in which they publish. New titles are constantly being added to the range, full details are available on request.